148873

Cherney.
Harry Somers.

BRIAN CHERNEY is a member of the Faculty of Music at McGill University, where he teaches theory and analysis, composition, and twentieth-century music history.

Harry Somers is one of Canada's leading composers, and one of the most original. In the 1950s he experimented with contrapuntal writing, serialism, and style juxtaposition; in more recent years he has been concerned with the development of new vocal resources and improvisation.

Harry Somers, a detailed study of the composer and his works, has been commissioned by the Canadian Music Centre as the first of a series, each volume of which will cover in depth the career and works of a major Canadian composer.

Within the framework provided by major biographical events, Brian Cherney traces Somers' development as a composer from 1939 to 1973 by analysing works from various stages in his career. He discusses in particular the influences on Somers of Bartók, Debussy, and Weinzweig, the interrelationships between his works, and his stylistic traits and compositional techniques. A chronological list of Somers' works is included, and, because of its importance, an entire chapter is devoted to the opera *Louis Riel*. In view of the scarcity of in-depth critical literature on Canadian composers, this thorough and objective book will be of interest to music students, professional musicians, composers, and the general musical public, both in Canada and abroad.

CANADIAN COMPOSERS / COMPOSITEURS CANADIENS

BRIAN CHERNEY

Harry Somers

UNIVERSITY OF TORONTO PRESS
TORONTO AND BUFFALO

© University of Toronto Press 1975
Toronto and Buffalo
Printed in Canada

Library of Congress Cataloging in Publication Data

Cherney, Brian.
  Harry Somers.
  (Canadian composers; 1) ISSN 0316-1293
  'Compositions by Harry Somers': p.
  Discography: p.
  Bibliography: p.
  Includes index.
  1. Somers, Harry Stewart, 1925–   I. Series.
  ML410.S6864C5 780'.92'4 [B]   75-15845
  ISBN 0-8020-5325-4

Permission from the following to use copyright material is gratefully acknowledged:

Berandol Music Limited: Passacaglia and Fugue for Orchestra, Symphony No. 1, *North Country*, *12 x 12*, Piano Concerto No. 2, Sonata No. 1 for Violin and Piano, Fantasia for Orchestra, *Lyric* for Orchestra, Five Concepts for Orchestra, Twelve Miniatures, *Evocations* (originally published by BMI Canada Limited, © 1969 assigned to Berandol Music Limited); and Five Songs for Dark Voice
Caveat Music Publishers Ltd.: *Stereophony* (© 1972 by Caveat Music Publishers Ltd., Toronto)
Doubleday & Company Inc.: haiku texts from *An Introduction to Haiku* by Harold G. Henderson (© 1958 by Harold G. Henderson)
Mavor Moore: synopsis of *Louis Riel* and extracts from the libretto of *Louis Riel* (© Libretto copyright by Mavor Moore, 1967)
C.F. Peters Corporation: Symphony for Woodwinds, Brass and Percussion (example 5.3) (copyright © 1969 by C.F. Peters Corporation, 373 Park Avenue South, New York, NY 10016, reprint permission granted by the publisher)
G.T. Sassoon and Viking Press: lines from 'Strangeness of Heart' by Siegfried Sassoon from *Collected Poems 1908–56* (London:Faber and Faber; New York: Viking Press, Inc.)
Gordon V. Thompson Limited: *God, the Master of this Scene*, 'Si J'avais le bateau,' and 'She's Like the Swallow'

To Harry Somers
on the occasion of his fiftieth birthday

Contents

viii Contents

General foreword / Avant-propos général

This book is the first in a projected series of studies of Canadian composers, commissioned by the Canadian Music Centre. As part of its effort to make Canadian composers' music more widely known at home and abroad, the Centre has assisted the research and writing of these studies, each designed to cover in some depth the career and works of an individual composer of particular prominence. It is our hope that the series will prove useful to many musicians and music lovers, and will thereby stimulate the performance and appreciation of the Canadian musical repertoire of our time.

Cet ouvrage fait partie d'une collection d'études commandées par le Centre de musique canadienne et consacrées aux compositeurs canadiens dont l'apport à la vie musicale mérite d'être souligné. Puisant à même une documentation fournie en grande partie par le Centre de musique canadienne, ces ouvrages s'adressent à tous ceux qui, au Canada comme à l'étranger, désirent se familiariser avec la production musicale canadienne contemporaine. Cette initiative rejoint les objectifs du Centre qui sont de faire connaître les compositeurs canadiens et de promouvoir l'exécution de leurs œuvres.

John Beckwith, Chairman
Publications Committee
Canadian Music Centre

Acknowledgments

I am grateful to a number of institutions and individuals for their assistance in preparing this volume. The reference library of the Canadian Broadcasting Corporation, BMI Canada Ltd, and the Canadian Music Centre made relevant material from their files available to me. Eric Aldwinckle, Victor Feldbrill, Reginald Godden, and John Weinzweig talked to me at length about their association with Somers over the years, and in some cases provided valuable documentary material. Richard Coulter, the CBC music producer, made available a large number of Somers' scripts for 'Music of Today,' and Michael Fram wrote to me at length about his collaboration with Somers during the fifties.

My special thanks go also to Keith MacMillan and Henry Mutsaers of the Canadian Music Centre, who took on the onerous task of furnishing me with all necessary scores and tapes (including all twelve volumes of *Louis Riel*), and assisted in numerous other ways.

The index was prepared by my wife Terri, who assisted me in numerous other ways during the research and writing of my work. I am also grateful to John Beckwith, the editor of the series, for his invaluable guidance and advice; to Margaret Bentley of the University of Toronto Press, under whose keen editorial supervision this book emerged; and to the composer John Fodi, who has copied the many musical examples.

Finally, and most important of all, I am indebted to Harry Somers, who not only talked with me at length about himself and his music, but made available to me a great deal of material, including manuscripts of works of the forties, without which chapters 1 and 2 would not have been complete.

This study is not intended to be a complete biography of Harry Somers; nor, in view of his prolific output, is it an exhaustive study of his music. Instead, I have concentrated on tracing his development as a composer over the years, selecting a number of works which illustrate various stages of that development. It is to be hoped that this study will provide a framework and point of departure for further exploration of his music.

Publication of this book has been made possible by a grant from the Humanities Research Council of Canada, using funds provided by the Canada Council, and a grant to the University of Toronto Press from the Andrew W. Mellon Foundation.

BC
Montreal
August 1974

Picture credits:

page xiii
By Evariste Desparois, *Saturday Night*, 18 July 1950
page xvii
By Ken Bell Art Associates Limited, courtesy of the National Ballet of Canada
page xviii
Courtesy of the Canadian Opera Company
page xix (bottom)
By Gillin, courtesy of BMI Canada Limited
page xx
Courtesy of BMI Canada Limited; bottom photograph by Robert C. Ragsdale Limited

Two Canadian student composers – Somers, left, and Clermont Pépin – at a Paris sidewalk café, 1950

Two annual meetings of the Canadian League of Composers. *Above*, 1955, at the Toronto home of John Beckwith: *standing, left to right*, Louis Applebaum, Samuel Dolin, Somers, Leslie Mann, Barbara Pentland, Andrew Twa, Harry Freedman, Udo Kasemets; *front, left to right*, Jean Papineau-Couture, John Weinzweig, John Beckwith. *Below*, 1966, at the Canadian Music Centre, Toronto, on the present site of the Metropolitan Toronto Public Library music division: *left to right*, Louis Applebaum, Morris Surdin, Harry Freedman, John Weinzweig, William McCauley, Somers, Jean Papineau-Couture, Srul Irving Glick, John Beckwith, Talivaldis Kenins, Norma Beecroft, Bruce Mather, István Anhalt, Helmut Kallmann (league archivist)

Friday, July 29, 1955

Dear Reg:

The 3rd movement is right! Went over it both in my minds ear and on the piano a number of times to-day. A long period of silence is the bridge between the 2nd and 3rd movements. Allowing sufficient time for the accumulated energy of the 2nd mvt. to be absorbed into the silence provides a perfect transition into the utter lonely simplicity of the piano.

I was more than a little awed yesterday to realize the stature of this concerto. Am looking forward to the next session.

Harry

1955 letter from Somers to Reginald Godden, who was soloist in the première of the Piano Concerto No. 2 (see text, page 72)

Poster designed by Graham Coughtry for the première of the chamber opera *The Fool*, Toronto 1956. The work by Somers and Michael Fram shared the double bill with *Une Mesure de silence* by Maurice and Marthe Blackburn

Two scenes from *The House of Atreus*, in the première production by the National Ballet of Canada, 1964. Choreography was by Grant Strate, and costume and set designs by Harold Town. Leading dancers were Lois Smith (Elektra), Yves Cousineau (Aegisthus), Earl Kraul (Orestes), and Jacqueline Ivings (Clytemnestra)

Two scenes from *Louis Riel*, in the première production by the Canadian Opera Company, 1967. Stage direction was by Leon Major, and set designs by Murray Laufer. *Above*, MacDougall and his party at the border (act I, scene i); *below*, Schultz (Peter Milne) confronts Riel (Bernard Turgeon) (act I, scene ii)

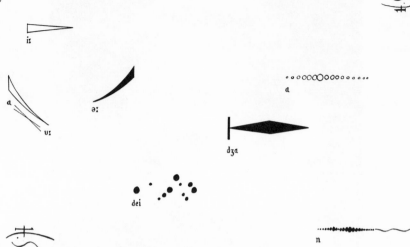

For the spring/summer 1973 issue of *Les Cahiers canadiens de musique/The Canada Music Book*, former students and colleagues of John Weinzweig contributed to a commemoration of Weinzweig's sixtieth birthday. Somers' 'birthday present' was this one-page untitled graphic composition

Reception following the concert of Canadian composers' works in Rome, May 1972, co-sponsored by the Nuova Consonanza and the Canadian Cultural Institute. *Left to right*, Somers, Mr and Mrs Egisto Macchi, Norma Beecroft, Victor Feldbrill (conductor of the concert), Mr and Mrs Mario Bertoncini, Mr and Mrs Franco Evangelisti (Mr Evangelisti is president of the Nuova Consonanza), Barbara Chilcott Somers

Harry Somers: two recent photographs

HARRY SOMERS

I
The early years

Rome, 17 May 1970
This morning I awoke at 4 AM. Looking out of the window I couldn't resist the first light. I got up, dressed, and went for a walk to the Capitol Hill across the beautiful Piazza designed by Michelangelo to a small park overlooking the ancient Forum, heart of Caesar's empire. There I watched the miracle of the day returning and my mind wandered through millenia of the earth's turning. Flocks of swallows wheeled, dipped, soared and fluttered above the ruins. A cat, one of the hundreds who live wild in these ancient sites, wandered by with a seeming careless stride, pausing now and then to gaze about, casually. You know, 'A morning stroll. No more than that. Birds? What birds? Oh those! Prrrrr. They don't interest me in the least! But of course, if one should just chance by ... well ... who am I to deny such gifts from the sky?'
On my return I saw a man fishing from the bank of the Tiber. I became aware of sounds suggesting themselves to my mind, and, re-entering the apartment, sketched them down.[1]

The night has always fascinated Harry Somers. To him, it is a strange, mysterious world of many faces. The cry of a loon echoing across a northern lake:

Loon cry,
Night call,

1 Letter to Eric Aldwinckle (published by permission of Harry Somers)

Mist, wreath of night,
Darkness, womb of night.
Above infinity of points of light.
Water, stillness,
Night sounds.
Loon cry
Echoes, haunts, dies
Loo ... Loo ...[2]

Or lone footsteps sounding in deserted streets (example 1.1). Within its stillness, the opportunity to reflect, to be alone, to compose (example 1.2).[3] But also a time for parties, friendships, and that special 'night music,' jazz, which he admires so much.

1.1 Five Songs for Dark Voice

As a child of four or five, he would wait until the family was asleep, then get up, dress carefully, and wander the streets until three or four in the morning, exploring the sounds and textures of the night. After one particularly strenuous ramble, the youthful adventurer prepared a light breakfast of toast before heading back to bed. A fatal miscalculation. Parents awoke (smelling toast), found Harry missing, called the police, and launched a futile search of the neighbourhood. Meanwhile, the object of all this coolly hid in some bushes and returned to bed when the coast was clear. When his parents returned, they discovered him in bed, fully dressed, boots and all, pretending to be asleep. After this, Harry's clothes were taken away at night to discourage any further nocturnal adventures.

2 Somers' text for the first of the *Evocations*, four songs for mezzo-soprano and piano (1966)
3 Early song, written by Somers in 1942 before he began composition studies with John Weinzweig (text by the composer)

1.2 *Stillness*: last section

The head of the household, James Russell Somers, was in the insurance business in Toronto. His grandfather had emigrated to Canada from Ireland after the potato famine of the 1840s. The next generation thrived in the new world – James W. Somers, OBE (Harry's grandfather), became City Clerk of Toronto and held that office until his death at the age of 84. His wife was of English and Dutch descent. Harry's mother, the former Ruth Brown, was descended on her father's side from Pennsylvania Quakers who had come to Ontario as United Empire Loyalists after the American Revolution. Her mother, on the other hand, could trace her Highland ancestry back to the eleventh century. James and Ruth Somers were married in 1919, after Mr Somers' return from France, where he had been a captain in the Canadian army. They had two sons, Robert (b. 1920) and Harry Stewart (b. 11 September 1925).

Harry appears to have been a lively, curious child, 'eating, tearing around, and playing games' (as he later wrote). He recalls that from a very early age he had a feeling for textures; at the age of three or four he would run outside in the morning 'filled with the sheer joy of seeing daylight and touching air.'[4] He also recalls that he enjoyed solitude and reflection. But there was no indication of a special interest in music. His

4 CBC radio documentary on Somers, prepared and narrated by Norma Beecroft and first broadcast on 14 April 1972 on 'Musicscope'

mother played the piano by ear. Through her he became acquainted with first world war songs and popular tunes of the day (including boogie-woogie – an important influence in his early writing). And he was exposed to the usual diet of class singing at Hodgson Public School. By the time he entered North Toronto Collegiate in 1938, his two main interests were sports and airplanes. He belonged to a group that met to discuss and build model airplanes. At this point, his musical accomplishments consisted of being able to whistle through the space between his front teeth, and playing *Chopsticks* on the piano (if someone else would play the lower part). The life of a tennis champion or hockey player seemed very attractive.

It was Mrs Somers' involvement in the Theosophical Society that was indirectly responsible for shifting the centre of interest in Harry's life. She began studying comparative religion during the thirties and conducted regular classes in the interpretation of the Bhagavad Gita at her home. In the summer of 1939, she and Harry were invited to spend a few weeks in Northern Ontario at the cottage of a friend from the study group (Mrs R. Daly). During a visit to a neighbouring cottage, Dr Max Broedel, a renowned medical artist, and his wife, both amateur musicians, began playing piano solos and duets on an old cottage upright. They played a variety of well-known pieces – Beethoven's *Moonlight* and *Pathétique* sonatas, waltzes by Brahms, and Mozart's *Eine kleine Nachtmusik*. For the impressionable young would-be tennis champion, this experience was 'an absolute shock. A spark ignited and I became obsessed with music. Almost from that instant I knew music would be my life, for better or for worse.'[5]

After returning to Toronto, he persuaded his parents to acquire an old upright from a relative and began studying piano with Dorothy Hornfelt, a neighbourhood music teacher. After only two years he was able to pass the Toronto Conservatory's grade VIII piano examination. He started to compose as soon as he began studying the piano. No doubt his discovery of the nineteenth- and early twentieth-century piano repertoire stimulated his curiosity and, coupled with his innate sensitivity to colour and texture, spurred him on to explore and re-create, in his own way, the musical materials encountered in that repertoire.

At first (1939–41) he composed almost exclusively for the piano. The pieces bear descriptive titles, such as *Northern Lights, Rain, Twilight,*

---

5 From an autobiographical sketch written in the late forties for Bailey Bird. I am indebted to Harvey Olnick for providing me with a copy of this sketch.

The Forest Glade, Fantasia of a Haunted Mill, Dream of Space, and Prelude *(Despair)*. Most of these are incomplete, although several appear to have undergone extensive revision. Their textures, which reflect the piano literature he was discovering at the time, range from simple melody with chordal accompaniment in the earliest pieces to arpeggio figurations with slowly moving chords or attenuated melodic accompaniment in later ones (for example, Nocturne or *The Forest Glade*). As could be expected, the formal structure is primitive. An idea (and it is evident that he was aware of the need to formulate distinctive, easily remembered ideas) is generally extended through direct repetition. At its worst, the result is constant sequential repetition of a short idea, or even a complete bar, as in Prelude *(Despair)*. This problem is encountered as late as 1947, in the opening of the Piano Concerto No. 1.

In retrospect, the real interest in these early compositional efforts lies in the development of the harmonic language. It must be remembered that as yet Somers had had no formal theory or composition instruction; from the beginning he had to discover his own language. (This type of thoroughly independent growth remained an important component of his later compositional development, no matter how many techniques or influences were assimilated into his creative bloodstream.) Consequently, in the early pieces traditional notions of chord progression and cadencing are lacking. Instead, there is an interest in the colouristic and sonorous possibilities of chords, for instance, the non-functional juxtaposition of simple triads (as in *Dream of Space*, where arpeggiated G minor, F major, and F minor triads are juxtaposed). The most interesting harmonic characteristic, in terms of future development, is a marked predilection, in the later works of this period, for parallel progressions of seventh, ninth, or eleventh chords, or of chords built in fourths or fifths. Examples of both of these can be seen in the excerpts from *Northern Lights* (c. 1941) in example 1.3, in both of which the influence of popular music and jazz is evident.

A few pieces from around the same time show certain characteristics of impressionist harmony and piano textures (although the only impressionist music he had studied at that time was *Claire de lune*). In *Rain*, a delicate pattern of alternating thirds between the hands, gradually descending from high to middle register of the piano, is interrupted by short arpeggio flourishes, with which the piece concludes. Much of the harmonic vocabulary of *Mists* (incomplete) consists of various types of seventh chords juxtaposed. Once an idea is stated it is simply repeated in a different register or extended sequentially.

1.3 *Northern Lights*: a/ bars 1–4; b/ bars 24–7

Among the later works of this period of independent exploration is the song *Stillness*, written in January of 1942. Not only is the harmonic language more sophisticated but the repetition of ideas is less rigid than in earlier pieces. The text (by the composer) conveniently divides the song into four parts. In the first, a tranquil mood is established by a slowly moving sequence of thirteenth chords over a recurring F pedal. The second section depicts the breeze in an obvious but effective way with light arabesque figurations in the piano. The third introduces a slow, shifting broken arpeggio figure of superimposed fifths in the left hand against parallel fourths in the right; this idea is literally lifted from the final portion of *Mists* (the self-borrowing evident in later works thus can be traced back to these early years – for example, part of the fifth movement of Five Concepts, 1961, reappears in *The House of Atreus*, 1963). The final section (see example 1.2) combines a few appropriate figures from earlier sections (for each repeated fragment of text) and at the end (on 'stillness') coalesces into the same chord that concludes the first part, including the voice's 'one soft note' – a B♮. Although naïve, the over-all effect is musical. Above all, the song demonstrates an ability to create and sustain contrasting moods through harmonic and pianistic resources.

It was during 1942 that Somers met the three men who were to play a

major role in his personal and musical development during the 1940s –
Eric Aldwinckle, Oxford-born artist and designer; Reginald Godden,
well-known concert pianist and teacher; and the composer John
Weinzweig, who was teaching at the Toronto (later Royal) Conservatory of Music. All three vividly recall being deeply impressed by the
sixteen-year-old's maturity, enthusiasm, and sincerity, as well as his
sensitivity to sounds and textures.

The first to meet him was Eric Aldwinckle, who was active in the
Theosophical Society and was introduced to Harry by Mrs Somers, after
the artist had given a lecture on aesthetics to her study group. Instead of
the awkward, shy teen-ager he had expected, relates Aldwinckle, he
was confronted with a strikingly handsome, self-assured man who pos-
sessed 'tremendous presence and dignity.' Despite a considerable difference in age, the two rapidly became close friends. Aldwinckle was
keenly interested in music, and something of a musician and composer
himself, possessing a piano and a record collection which offered further
stimulation to Harry's ever-broadening musical horizons. A short time
later, just before going overseas as an official Canadian war artist with
the RCAF, Aldwinckle arranged for his young friend to meet Reginald
Godden, who was then teaching at the Toronto Conservatory. Somers
officially studied piano with Godden for only one year (1942–3) but the
two have remained close friends ever since. A number of the early piano
works were dedicated to Godden: *Strangeness of Heart, Étude* (1943),
Three Sonnets (1946), *Solitudes* (1947). It was Godden who gave the first
performance of the Piano Concerto No. 2 in 1956.

Godden realized that the young pianist-composer's creative spark
would probably be stifled by a dry, academic approach to the teaching of
music theory and composition. He sent Somers to see John Weinzweig
who, although he taught at the conservatory, was regarded by many
established musicians as a fifth columnist, bent on destroying the traditional nineteenth-century musical language. In order fully to ap-
preciate the significance of Somers' contact with Weinzweig, one must
remember that in the early forties Toronto's musical life was deeply
rooted in the nineteenth century. Except for the occasional work by
Ravel, Debussy, Sibelius, or Vaughan Williams (who were considered
modern), the music of the twentieth century rarely crept into the
Toronto Symphony's repertoire. Two of the early ballet scores of
Stravinsky– *The Firebird* and *Petrushka* – had reached Toronto only five
years earlier (under the baton of Stravinsky himself). Modern Russian
composers such as Prokofiev or Shostakovich were considered daring.

Reginald Godden, who played a good deal of modern French and Russian piano music during those years, recalls the icy reception which greeted a recital of his at the conservatory in 1944 which consisted entirely of twentieth-century music. John Weinzweig's String Quartet No. 1, a romantic, traditional work written in 1938, was considered a modern piece. The music of Schoenberg and his school or of innovators like Varèse or Bartók was unknown to any but a few like Weinzweig who had studied outside the country. The music of the older generation of composers then active in Canada – highly gifted, thoroughly trained men like Champagne, MacMillan, Willan, and Smith – was firmly rooted in the late nineteenth-century European tradition. The notion of a 'Canadian composer' did not exist. As Helmut Kallmann points out in *A History of Music in Canada 1534–1914*,[6] the composers of Weinzweig's generation had to bypass the example of the older generation and seek guidance from the developments of European and American music of the twenties and thirties.

John Weinzweig was perhaps the only music teacher in Toronto at that time (with the possible exception of Barbara Pentland) who could have given Somers the background and impetus he needed. While studying at the Eastman School of Music in 1938, he had become acquainted with a number of early twentieth-century scores – in particular Berg's *Lyric Suite* and Stravinsky's *Rite of Spring* – works which were to alter profoundly the direction of his writing. By 1942 he was using a highly personal technique of linear serialism to achieve coherence and formal logic in structures which had no basis in conventional tonality or form (e.g. the Violin Sonata of 1941). Above all, as a teacher of some three years' standing, he was evidently aware of the need to tailor compositional training to meet the requirements and personality of each individual student.

Weinzweig set up an intensive program of study to develop Somers' craft. After covering traditional harmony (in about five months), he proceeded with analysis and creative exercises. The analysis covered a wide range of music – Bach, Beethoven, Wagner, Debussy, Stravinsky, Schoenberg's string quartets and *Pierrot Lunaire*, Berg's Lyric Suite and Violin Concerto, Webern's Opus 5, and Bartók quartets, among others.[7] From Weinzweig Somers learned to examine a score objectively, in the realization that 'quality judgment will inhibit you from being able to analyse a score.'[8]

6 University of Toronto Press 1960
7 Somers 'Letter to Lee Hepner' 94 (Short titles refer to works in the bibliography.)
8 'Musicscope' documentary 1972

The written exercises were designed to develop skill in a number of areas – instrumentation, application of a series, and, above all, writing a good melodic line. This is extremely important in tracing the origins of Somers' later preoccupation with line. Weinzweig believed that if all musical parameters were built into a single extended melodic line within a set metre, the most difficult compositional problems could be dealt with – continuity, contour, instrumental colour, pitch organization, and so on. This could later be expanded into two-part contrapuntal writing. The basis of pitch organization in those exercises was a twelve-note series. The use of a series, Weinzweig believed, sharpened the sense of continuity and the awareness of the personalities of intervals, ensured stylistic unity, and served as a basis for constructing thematic units. At that time he did not believe that, for teaching purposes, the series should be the basis of vertical aggregates as well as linear continuities.

The first large work written under Weinzweig's guidance and, in effect, Somers' Opus 1, was the String Quartet No. 1, written in 1943 and dedicated to Eric Aldwinckle. Even in an abstract work like a string quartet, the descriptive tendencies so much in evidence in most of Somers' works of the forties are present: the third movement bears the inscription 'Outwardly I smile, while inwardly I weep.' Although the work retains certain characteristics of the previous piano pieces, it reveals the astonishing progress made in less than a year under Weinzweig's supervision. The turgid chromaticism and textural density of the opening measures recall the opening of Schoenberg's String Quartet Opus 7, but other indications of a stylistic lineage are conspicuously absent. In fact, the seeds of certain important characteristics of the later Somers are already present.

One of the most impressive aspects of the quartet as a whole is the treatment of motivic ideas. An idea is not merely repeated (as in the early piano pieces); characteristic intervals, fragments, and even the general contour of an idea may pervade an entire movement. In example 1.4, several figures (b, c, and d) are shown which derive from the main thematic idea of the first movement (a). The result of the exercises in building and extending melodic lines can be seen throughout the quartet, especially in the outer movements. In example 1.5, an excerpt from the first movement, the first violin line, which shows the contour of the movement's main theme, rises in two stages to a climax in bars nine and ten of the example. The falling semitone at the peak of phrases relates to the D♭–c at the crest of the main theme. After eight pitches of the chromatic scale have been exposed, the line doubles back, then

1.4 String Quartet No. 1: first movement: a/ bars 1–3, main thematic idea;
b/bars 18–20; c/ bars 35–8; d/ bars 43–7

moves on to unfold the remaining four pitches at the climax. This is not
to suggest that the work is serial; there is no connection between the
order of pitches in example 1.5 and that in other lines which have a
similar profile (for example, the main theme of the fourth movement,
whose first three pitches outline a G minor triad).

1.5 String Quartet No. 1: first movement, bars 111–20

The ostinato is already an important element in Somers' language by
this time. In example 1.5 there are three ostinati of different lengths
which serve as accompaniment to the slower moving melodic line.
Ostinati are used in all movements to fulfil a variety of functions. At
the beginning of the opening movement, a fragment of the main theme
(marked x in example 1.4a) becomes an ostinato in the viola. In the

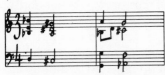

1.6 a/ String Quartet No. 1: second movement, bars 1–5; b/ *Stillness*: bars 1–2

slow movement the ostinato is a regularly recurring chord progression accompanying a rather sad, static melody in the first violin. The last movement contains a fast-moving ostinato pattern of eleven different pitches (later subjected to various transformations, as well as a more exclusively rhythmic ostinato which helps build excitement at the end). The superimposition of two or more layers moving at different speeds is one of the most important characteristics of Somers' music right through to *Kyrie*.

Harmonically, the writing in areas of thin texture or declamatory chordal outbursts (as in the first movement) is more successful than in thicker quasi-linear sections, such as the first seventeen bars of the first movement, where the vertical results of voice movement – unrelated triads, seventh chords, or simply thirds – seem uncontrolled. In passages which are vertically conceived, the earlier trait of parallel motion (often chromatic) of seventh, ninth, or eleventh chords is much in evidence. The slow movement begins with a pattern of triads descending chromatically (example 1.6a); when the melody enters in bar three, it obscures each accompanying triad (except at the very beginning) by adding a dissonance. The arrival on a G minor triad 'obscured' by an A in the upper part (marked with an asterisk) is remarkably similar to the opening of *Stillness* (example 1.6b). Similarly, the end of the first movement, the main idea of which (see example 1.4a) is essentially in F minor, concludes with an F minor chord 'obscured' by a B in one voice. This is not unlike the ending of Five Songs for Dark Voice (1956) – an E♭ minor chord with an added E♮. The addition of dissonant elements to an essentially tonal or triadic framework often accounts for the bitter-sweet quality of many of the early works.

The formal structure of individual movements of the quartet shows a tendency to avoid set formulae, although generally a loose ABA or abridged rondo-like scheme can be discerned. The scheme of the first movement, for instance, is ABCA'DA; sections B, C, and D begin with thinner textures than A and work up to climactic rhythmic reiterations of chords. Even in this early work, then, there is a sense of the dramatic possibilities of the building up and releasing of tension. It was not really until *North Country* (1948) that Somers succeeded in building tension over a single unified arc, rather than through a mosaic-like series of sections. The general emotional tone of the quartet (and indeed much of the later music) is serious and intense, with a tendency to indulge in melodramatic, declamatory outbursts. He later said of this period, 'the general development was through an intention at the expressive, using sound to somehow relate that intensity of feeling that you have, somehow make the intangible link, I suppose, between internal response and another person's consciousness.'[9]

The next major work, *Testament of Youth* (Piano Sonata No. 1), the outer movements of which were written in the fall of 1945, is clearly foreshadowed in several piano works written before and after the string quartet. Some measure of the progress made in one year can be gained by comparing *Strangeness of Heart* (written in December of 1942) with *Étude* (December 1943), *Flights of Fancy* (January 1944) and *Dark and Light* (March 1944). *Strangeness of Heart* was inspired by Siegfried Sassoon's poem of the same title, which expresses a fear of losing child-hood receptiveness and sensitivity to the beauty of nature. Somers attempted to capture the feeling of the last four lines of the poem:

When I have lost those simple spells that stirred
My being with an untranslated song,
Let me go home for ever; I shall have heard
Death; I shall know that I have lived too long.[10]

One notes here the suggestion of musical ideas originating from extra-musical experiences; until the Piano Sonata No. 2 nearly all of his music

9 Ibid

10 Siegfried Sassoon *Collected Poems 1908–56* (London, Faber 1947; New York, Viking Press, Inc.) 181

bears descriptive titles.[11] But the poem also calls to mind the *raison d'être* of *Testament of Youth*. (The latter work was an expression of Somers' grief and outrage at the death, in a German U-boat raid during the closing days of the war, of a close friend, Dudley Garrett, Jr, a vital young man capable of experiencing those 'simple spells.') The musical connection between the two works is striking. In both, the sound of the major seventh chord (with major or minor third) predominates, especially at points of high emotional intensity. In the later work, a calm, slowly moving melodic line over an arpeggiated bass, towards the end of the first movement, recalls the opening section of *Strangeness of Heart*. But despite the quaint harmonic colour achieved by juxtaposing various types of inverted seventh chords (in the arpeggiated ostinato accompaniment in the outer sections), *Strangeness of Heart* shares the problem of over-repetition of ideas already noted in earlier piano pieces, and the rhetorical climax of the middle section is emotionally inflated.

The piano pieces written about a year later show considerably more sophistication in the kind of material used, the organization, and the understanding of pianistic idiom. The most ambitious, and in some ways the most revealing, is *Étude*, written in December 1943. The piece is built around fairly difficult passage work involving perfect fourths moving chromatically in one hand against a contrasting pattern in the other. This would be mere finger exercise were it not for the dramatic interruptions of the passage work, most extensively by a gradually rising melody which reaches a climax on a repeated, declamatory c♯ in octaves. This and an earlier, more extensive declamatory interruption foreshadow the dramatic declamatory gestures in the outer movements of *Testament of Youth*. *Étude* ends with an accelerando on one note:

In later works, the accelerando on one note (usually written into the notation) becomes an important ingredient of many climactic points and assumes a motivic significance of its own in *Stereophony* (1963).

11 See also the letter from Rome at the beginning of this chapter. In program notes for his piano recital on 13 March 1948 (consisting entirely of his own music), Somers wrote briefly about his use of descriptive titles: 'These titles are merely signposts indicating the direction the music has come from. In no instance are they to be taken literally as representing a particular thing, or that the music is trying to represent a particular thing. The important thing is that the titles are symbols.'

1.7 *Moon Haze*: bars 12–15

Flights of Fancy (written in January 1944 and dedicated to Eric Aldwinckle) is made up of three short pieces – 'Dance,' 'A Mood,' and 'Moon Haze.' They are all delicate, quiet mood pieces, completely lacking in the dramatic contrasts and rhetorical outbursts of other works of the period. The last two are, in some ways, more experimental than the other piano pieces of the early forties. 'Moon Haze,' for example, is the most 'impressionistic' of all the early works. With the sostenuto and damper pedals down through the piece, three static layers are superimposed in the low, middle, and high registers of the piano: in order of appearance, a four-note ostinato, a sad, floating melody consisting of all twelve pitches of the chromatic scale, and a faster-moving arabesque-like figure in the extreme high register. The fact that the melody contains all twelve pitches is no accident – in a brief sketch for the piece the melody's pitches are set down under the word 'series.' This may be the earliest statement of a complete twelve-note series in Somers' free compositions.[12] Example 1.7 shows the interaction of the three layers from the point at which they come together.

The first period of study with John Weinzweig was interrupted after about a year, when, late in 1943, both men joined the armed forces. Because of his interest in airplanes, Harry joined the Royal Canadian Air Force, but never saw active duty. Instead, he was sent back and forth to various training camps in Manitoba and Ontario, marching, cleaning equipment, marching, working in the laundry, and marching some more. In the early spring of 1944 he wrote to Eric Aldwinckle (who was then in London, preparing to leave for the invasion of Normandy) to express his confusion and dismay at the circumstances in which he found himself. Aldwinckle recalls that the letter, now lost, ended with

12 He had been using a series in exercises, chiefly for purposes of melodic writing.

the question 'Why am I here?' In reply, Aldwinckle wrote a letter in the form of a fable in blank verse.[13] The fable, ostensibly a dialogue between an older and a younger vase, functions on several levels of meaning. On one level it portrays, from the point of view of a work of art (specifically a vase but by extension any work of art), the relationship between the artist and the work of art. On another, it traces the growth of a work of art (and by extension, the artist himself) from its beginnings in the mind of the artist ('I was his thought form') through the slow, painful stages of realization to the final object existing independently in the material world as a 'record of its creator.' Particularly striking is the contrast between the fluid, rich world of the imagination and the 'coarser and clumsier' material world ('I [the older vase] could see that I would be terribly confined in the material world outside'). The final section of the fable seems addressed directly to Somers:

You [the younger vase] too, will grow in the passage of time
to the consciousness of your own spirit.
You will remember what you have been through
and where you have come from,
and this,
and this only,
will show you why you are here.

The reply to Aldwinckle, dated 5 May 1944, provides a remarkable portrait of the Harry Somers of 1944:

... Your blank verse came. ... truthfully it is an inspiration in itself and to those who read it. I was so struck that I must have sat (I am not sure how long exactly) a couple of hours meditating on it, absorbing it. So beautiful. Delicately cut. It's as though you have moulded statues out of the substance of the air. ... I felt the joy as if I had written a sound as I heard it. For some strange reason it has filled me with courage, purpose, hope again, for I am very young. Being away from the piano and active composition, seeing people as some of them are, being where sensitivity is suffocated, foreseeing the chaos which will be the future of chaos, feeling its searching of the youth to-day I sometimes become discouraged.

Then you create a composition and it turns my eyes ahead to the true reality.

13 Published, along with another fable, by the University of Toronto Press in 1950 under the title *Two Fables* but no longer available. I am indebted to Eric Aldwinckle for making this and Somers' reply available to me.

> My direction is regained.
> You are the true artist.
> All I can say now, is that I hope someday to offer you in my music a portion of what you have given me and others ...

Somers' feelings about the 'youth of to-day,' expressed in general terms in this letter and subsequently given a dimension of personal grief by the death of his friend Dudley Garrett, Jr, found expression, as previously mentioned, in *Testament of Youth* (Piano Sonata No. 1). Completed in October 1945 and dedicated to the memory of Dudley Garrett, Jr, *Testament of Youth* is a grand, romantic work, with rich, full sonorities, maximum use of the entire range of the keyboard, and difficult passage work; in terms of piano writing, it is effective and convincing.[14]

The flamboyant instrumental writing is a vital component of the character of the music. The outer movements are highly dramatic, with abrupt contrasts and rhetorical, passionate, even angry outbursts of intense emotion. Despite the fact that the many contrasts tend to create a multitude of small sections, each with a new figuration or idea, the work is remarkably cohesive. This is due to two main factors: the consistent use of certain harmonic material (presented at the beginning of the first movement) and tight motivic control, especially in the first movement. The main pitch centres of the work are Eb and D, and much of the smaller-level interval structure reflects this relationship. The clearest tonal statement comes in the first five bars of the first movement; in this respect it reminds one of the E minor chord at the beginning of the String Quartet No. 2. It differs from the quartet, however, in that the Eb tonality is never recalled as clearly again in the course of the sonata, although the pitch-class itself occurs prominently again – as the bass of the final chord of the first movement, and as a pedal at the beginning of the second, for instance. The root of the final chord of the work (a major seventh chord) is D. A predominant mood of conflict is established immediately within the opening twenty bars, not only by the clash of major sevenths and minor ninths, but by the collision of chords built in thirds and fourths. The effect is powerful and strident (example 1.8).[15] One of the most important intervals is the major seventh, generally filled in with a third or fifth or sometimes a tritone. This sound permeates much of the Sonata, particularly the outer move-

14 The slow movement was actually written in December of 1944 and dedicated to Reginald Godden. It is entitled 'A Fragment' in early lists of works.
15 Note that example 1.8 is the first of several in this volume in Somers' own hand.

1.8 *Testament of Youth*: bars 1–5 (in the composer's hand)

ments. One notes as well frequent use of parallel progressions of bare fourths or fifths (example 1.9), although nowhere as consistently as in later works where these progressions dominate the vertical sonority and produce a characteristic 'Somers' sound.

A significant feature of the work is the conscious transformation of a small interval cell (marked x in example 1.9) first introduced in the

1.9 *Testament of Youth*: first movement: a/ bar 29; b/ bar 38; c/ bar 52; third movement: d/ bars 70–4

slow introduction to the first movement. This becomes the basis of a driving rhythmic figure in the latter part of the first movement, and fragments also appear in the second and third movements. The relentless, somewhat brutal later part of the first movement is interrupted twice by serene, floating melodic lines accompanied by arpeggiated figures whose triadic implications mix strangely with those of the melodic line. The first melody line contains eleven different pitches; the second, all twelve pitches of the chromatic scale. Also, the extended flamboyant passage near the end of the first movement consists of successive transpositions of a twelve-note series which in itself begins with figure z of the interval cell x. At this stage of Somers' development, the linear statement of a complete series is unusual.

There are many other features of this piece one could mention: the strong rhythmic vitality; the ostinato bass patterns combined with slower-moving, static melodic lines, especially in the last movement; or the inactive, expressive melody of the second movement, with its falling semitone (a component, marked y, of interval cell x). This is one of the earliest examples of the falling semitone figure, which recurs throughout the fifties and has associations of pain or sadness. All in all, *Testament of Youth* is a remarkable accomplishment for a composer who had just turned twenty-one and had been away from composition for two years. Despite the fact that its emotional nerve endings are exposed and sometimes raw, it is a convincing piece of music. During the years 1946–8 it was often performed by the composer himself; several people who first met Somers in those years, including Keith MacMillan and Victor Feldbrill, recall the powerful impression his performance made on them. Reginald Godden believed that it was 'a landmark in creative music in this country.'[16]

In late October of 1945, soon after being released from the armed services, Somers and Eric Aldwinckle went camping in northern Ontario, as Aldwinckle relates, 'to paint God, peace, quietude, and the sounds of nature.' It is interesting to note that both were to produce works of art which directly or indirectly reflected their experience of the

16 Quoted in a CBC press and information sheet of February 1947. A review by John H. Yocom in *Saturday Night* 10 May 1947, 34, gives an idea of the strong impression made by the work: '... [*Testament of Youth*] had been worked out on major dimensions and was completely effective melodically, harmonically, and in over-all plan. The angry chords of the Largo, the utter simplicity of the melody in the contrasting Adagio, and the patterned bass of the third movement out of which grew again those angry chords were important elements in a most impressive work, played by Godden.'

northern Ontario environment. Over the next two years, Aldwinckle completed a series of six paintings entitled 'Northern Ontario Poems,' in each of which the torso of a man is superimposed on a particular aspect of the landscape. In the fall of 1948, Somers wrote *North Country*, a suite for string orchestra – conceived as a piece of 'absolute' music, yet marvellously suggestive of the qualities of that vast, silent land made famous by the Group of Seven.

2
The apprenticeship

I was out of touch with things happening in Europe –
I had to learn my own way.
Harry Somers, CBC radio documentary 1972

In the fall of 1945, after his release from the armed services, Somers resumed composition studies with John Weinzweig and began studying piano with Weldon Kilburn. Until the summer of 1948, he seems to have regarded composition and performance as equally important, complementary facets of his musical life. Despite his intention to become a concert pianist, these were years of intense compositional activity. From January of 1946 to September of 1949 he produced thirteen substantial works, several of which are still widely known today.

Certain elements present in works already discussed can also be discerned in these: motoric, patterned figures, often ostinato-like (for example, the last movement of the Piano Sonata No. 2); the presentation and rhythmic transformation of distinctive interval cells (for example, the Piano Sonata No. 2, Scherzo for Strings); and the extended, often intense melodic line, moving through small intervals in the general shape of an arc. These lines have two kinds of accompaniment: the fragmentary interjection (as in the slow movement of the Woodwind Quintet or at the end of the Rhapsody for Violin and Piano), or a rapid ostinato, which serves as a foil to the slower-moving melodic line (as in the last movement of the Piano Sonata No. 2 or 'West Wind'). As for harmonic language, there is a notable increase in the parallel movement of chords built in fourths and fifths; these are especially noticeable in piano writing (for instance, in the Rhapsody for Violin and Piano). The fourth seems also to have been a favourite melodic interval – as in the motivic cell of the first movement of *North Country*. Although it is difficult to generalize, tonal references (i.e., clear vertical or horizontal triadic configurations, but not traditional chord progressions) appear to have tension-releasing associations in many works, not only of this period, but well into the fifties. In the Rhapsody, for instance, after the first climax, the violin unwinds in a sad melodic soliloquy with a clear D minor tonal centre. And in the song 'Look Down Fair Moon,' the D minor triad is associated with the 'fair moon,' while 'faces ghastly swollen' is accompanied by an augmented triad with added minor second.

Approximately half of the works between 1946 and 1949 are descriptive in some sense, although one notes that extra-musical associations became more objective, detached, and peripheral than in works before 1946.[1] Although intense emotional states are occasionally projected in somewhat inflated, rhetorical gestures (as in the Piano Concerto No. 1, or the Piano Sonata No. 2), there is a gradual discovery of other, more subtle ways of building, controlling, and balancing emotional drive. *North Country* is an important milestone in this respect. Imitative contrapuntal textures play a relatively minor role in the music of this period; there are brief 'fugal' encounters in the Scherzo for Strings, at the end of the Piano Concerto No. 1, and in the Woodwind Quintet, for instance, but nothing to suggest the extent to which fugue occupied Somers during the fifties. The second movement of the Suite for Percussion, a fugue for tom-toms alone, is an isolated case. Generally, however, one can discern a shift towards thinner, more contrapuntal textures involving two or three (rarely more) individual but interdependent lines or distinct elements of a linear nature, as in the Scherzo for Strings, the Woodwind Quintet, or *North Country*. But generalizations are hazardous; much of the writing in the Rhapsody for Violin and Piano (written just before *North Country*) consists of a single melodic line, sometimes doubled in unisons or octaves, accompanied by chunky chords. It is equally difficult to generalize about such things as formal

1 In program notes for his piano recital of 13 March 1948, Somers wrote that in the future he intended to use descriptive titles 'only in very special instances': 'I have discovered that it is very dangerous to use a title. People tend to hang on to a title for dear life, using it to visualize countless objects which they think the music represents. Consequently the music becomes a sort of second hand medium for painting or literature, instead of a medium in itself.'

2.1 Sketches for Orchestra: 'Horizon,' bars 1–6

structure or pitch organization in works of varying dimensions and instrumental combinations. In the later 1940s Somers was exploring a variety of techniques, with a view to finding the best solution for each work as it evolved, instead of using universally valid methods and formats.

Notwithstanding this diversity of approaches, one of the most important traits of Somers' mature style – the build-up and release of tension over a wide arc – can be traced back to the works of this period. Although the most characteristic and striking instance of this device occurs in the first movement of *North Country*, an earlier attempt can be seen in the first movement of Somers' first orchestral work, Sketches for Orchestra ('Horizon,' 'Shadows,' and 'West Wind'). Written in 1946, 'Horizon' is one of the most revealing works of the period. It not only shows influences and techniques that he was exploring, but also indicates the nature of things to come. The entire piece – a single, intense build-up to a climax – is constructed around nine gradually compressed statements of a sixteen-note theme first presented in thirds by muted cellos (example 2.1). The upper part of this theme consists of a complete twelve-note series, with four additional pitches (marked x). In the second statement the series is presented twice: first, a semitone higher, then in retrograde at the original pitch level. One might expect a young composer to use the series quite rigidly. Typically for Somers, this is not the case. In the second statement, an E♮ is substituted for an E♭, the fourth pitch in the series, forming an E minor configuration with the following three pitches. In the succeeding seven statements, the series is shortened and considerably reshuffled, although the order of segments is retained. As the statements become shorter, a three-pitch cell from figure x completely replaces the original series. At the climax of the movement, only the retrograde-inversion of this cell is heard (having moved by then into the violins). Such a flexible use of the series is highly prophetic of works of the later forties in which the series may be used intact for longer periods, but is eventually broken into smaller segments which are treated freely. The constant repetition of a slowly moving melodic idea suggests passacaglia technique. In this sense 'Horizon' anticipates the Passacaglia and Fugue for Orchestra of 1954.

The series does not provide material for the two shorter melodic ideas of 'Horizon' – one first presented imitatively by the woodwinds; the other, more tense, by the violins as the climax is prepared. Tension is skilfully increased by shortening the passacaglia-like idea, gradually adding more orchestral weight, and moving into a higher register. Bass and percussion are saved for sharp, rhythmic jabs at the very climax – again, a detail which foreshadows similar devices in orchestral works of the fifties. The influence of Weinzweig in 'Horizon' is unmistakable – in the economy of texture, in the use of the orchestra (even at the climax the texture is basically two-part), and in the way in which the small interval cell of the woodwind melody is repeated in rhythmically varied form.[2] Space does not permit a detailed discussion of 'Shadows' and 'West Wind,' both of which are as revealing as 'Horizon.' For instance, the opening of 'Shadows' is an extended, sad, beautifully shaped English horn melody, dissonantly set off by isolated, halting figures (moving largely by parallel fourths) in a high register of the first violins. A mood is at once established – tentative, lonely, tense, as if balanced on the edge of a precipice.

As already indicated, the piano was Somers' main outlet for composition during 1946 and 1947. The largest work for solo piano, the Piano Sonata No. 2, completed on 30 November 1946, consists of three movements marked Lento, Scherzando, and Allegro. The heavy, extensive third movement is preceded by two lighter, thinner, and more compact ones. The opening of the first movement (example 2.2) is the most highly organized two-part writing one encounters until *North Country*. The second movement marks the earliest appearance of the Somers scherzo – thinly textured, full of rhythmic vitality, and built around the juxtaposition of two or three short ideas which are expanded and permutated until a high point is reached. A favourite device is the octave doubling of a rapidly moving melodic figure at or after a point of climax. The third movement is in many ways a more developed and dramatic counterpart to the third movement of *Testament of Youth*. It is extremely difficult technically, with wide leaps, powerful chords, and many passages in which the pianist must simultaneously manage three

2 In 'Letter to Lee Hepner' 95, Somers wrote: 'In his own music Weinzweig has always had certain idiosyncrasies. One in particular is the working around particular 'cells' of notes, constantly varying their individual shapes and durations like someone turning an object around and around to reveal all its shapes and colours.'

2.2 Piano Sonata No. 2: first movement, bars 1–16 (in the composer's hand)

layers moving at different speeds. Much of the vitality here results from driving ostinato figures (the first of which is probably based on boogie-woogie). Against these are slower-moving ideas, sometimes coherent, extended melody or shorter, static fragments which are interrupted by a brief flourish. The over-all structure is a factor of the dramatic build-up and release of tension over extended periods.

The largest and possibly weakest work of these years is the three-movement Piano Concerto No. 1, written in 1947 and first performed in 1949 by the composer himself, accompanied by the Royal Conservatory Symphony Orchestra under Ettore Mazzoleni. The rambling and diffuse first movement is more than twice as long as the third. It has grand romantic gestures – sweeping emphatic themes,[3] bravura chromatic octave passages, quasi-dramatic recapitulation of themes in octaves, accompanied by broken arpeggio figures – but there is a noticeable lack of a real dramatic confrontation between soloist and orchestra. The third movement, on the other hand, is more compact, and has a greater sense of direction, moving towards a cadenza which features a series of eleven extended virtuoso passages over tremolo chords in the strings. The concerto appears to have furnished several ideas for *North Country*, written the following year. The broken eighth-note accompaniment figures in the first movement of the later work, as well as trill figures at the beginning of the *più mosso* section of the third movement, can be found in the first movement of the concerto (the trill figure is exactly the

3 The main, introductory theme begins with an eleven-note series, but, as in the first movement of the Piano Sonata No. 2, small interval cells are used as the basis of later motives.

same in both works and was suggested by the trills at the beginning and end of the second movement of Bartók's Fifth String Quartet).

In retrospect, the Piano Concerto No. 1 seems to have been a catharsis of sorts, one last fling at the grand external trappings of nineteenth-century romanticism.[4] Even in the context of works written immediately before and after, it is anachronistic. The Scherzo for Strings, written in April of 1947 (before the concerto) is a cheerful, attractive work, notable for its transparent textures, rhythmic vitality, and skilful manipulation of motives. The length and accentuation patterns of melodic phrases are extremely flexible with relation to the underlying metric framework of $\frac{3}{4}$ or $\frac{4}{4}$. The work is generally mellow harmonically; chords are basically triadic, with added major seconds or perfect fourths, while the individual lines themselves have tonal implications, although no specific key areas are emphasized.[5] Effective use is made throughout of contrasts in weight, in particular between a 'concertino' solo quartet and the full string orchestra. This, as well as unison tutti passages, and rhythmic figures like

♫ ♫♫ ♫

suggest baroque influences, although imitative devices, which are so important in post-1950 works, play a minimal role here.

Two little-known works of the later forties, Suite for Percussion (1947) and the Woodwind Quintet (1947–8) permit glimpses of certain facets of Somers' musical personality which do not appear in other generally known works of the same period.

The Suite for Percussion (scored for piano and four tom-toms) was written in the late fall of 1947 for performance on a program called 'Variations on a Theme' at the Arts and Letters Club, Toronto, on December 9–11 of the same year.[6] Its five movements are entitled 'Decla-

---

4 In a review in *Saturday Night* 31 May 1949, 26, John Beckwith wrote: 'In the Somers Concerto there was the ... case of an ultra-expressive and ultra-primitivistic essay on the collapse of civilization, in essence the most romantic piece of the evening by far ... we are sincerely concerned to see him striving so heroically in the field of musical editorializing, a field which, never fertile, has been pretty well exhausted by now.'

5 It is interesting to note that later works of a 'lighter' nature also have strong tonal references. Somers believes that these permit associations not possible with a non-tonal, more dissonant language.

6 In the score, the work is entitled Essays for Percussion; on the concert program it is Suite for Percussion. I am indebted to Reginal Godden for making his copy of the score – probably the only one extant – available to me. The Arts and Letters Club, Toronto, essentially a luncheon club for men interested in the arts, was founded in 1910, and has had a tradition of presenting plays, concerts, art shows, speakers, and so on.

2.3 Suite for Percussion: 'Declamation,' bars 8–13

mation,' Fughetta (for tom-toms alone), 'A Bit of Dust,' Adagio, and 'Fast Blues.' Except for the Fughetta, the tom-toms largely play a supporting role in the form of steady rhythmic ostinati, against which the piano introduces irregular, asymmetrical rhythms of its own.

In this work, everything superfluous has been removed – the main element is rhythm, and this is emphasized by working with single lines (often doubled in octaves) or by straight chord reiteration. In 'Declamation,' for instance, a characteristic gesture of later Somers can be observed: tense, fragmented, static melodic figures, which gather momentum by briefly accelerating before bursting into a falling second, most characteristically a minor second (example 2.3). In the last movement of *North Country* the same kind of material is rearranged and charged with more nervous energy (but lacks the regular metrical framework of an attack on the first beat of each measure). The brief fugue, for four tom-toms alone, foreshadows the second movement of *Five Concepts for Orchestra* (1961). In the earlier piece Somers uses simple, distinctive rhythmic ideas which can be easily remembered and broken into smaller units. The texture is well thought out with contrasts of weight and timbre, stretto entries, and an effective build-up of tension towards the end. 'Fast Blues' is probably the 'jazziest' piece Somers has ever written: – in the piano a 'boogie-woogie' ostinato bass pattern underlies a somewhat rhapsodic right hand part which includes tremolos, glissandi, and short reiterated rhythmic figures. A movement like this (example 2.4)

2.4 Suite for Percussion: 'Fast Blues,' bars 28–33

clearly points to the jazz origins of similar ostinato bass figures in the first three piano sonatas.

The four-movement Woodwind Quintet (composed between October of 1947 and May of 1948) offers a unique example of Somers' use of serialism before 1950. It would appear that for him, at this stage, there were two classes of compositions – 'student works' (like the Woodwind Quintet), which use serial techniques of pitch organization to a limited extent, and 'free' works (like the Rhapsody for Violin and Piano, *North Country*, or the Suite for Harp and Chamber Orchestra), in which the series, if used at all, is stated only once, as a source from which interval cells are drawn.[7] All movements of the quintet except the Andante are light-hearted, with attractive, bouncy rhythmic ideas well suited to the combination, and thin textures enhanced by contrasts and witty exchanges between individuals and pairs (often doubled in thirds). Generally, the writing is linear, with considerable use of various contrapuntal devices: short points of imitations (à la Bartók), canon (especially just before the return of the opening section in the first movement), and the presentation of an idea in mirror with itself. The work is, in several senses, the most 'neo-classic' of all the early works.

Example 2.5 illustrates the manner in which pitches are derived from the series. In both cases – the opening chord sequence of the first movement (example 2.5b) and the first part of the main melodic idea (example 2.5c) – the interval of the perfect fourth, not the exact succession of pitches in the series, guides pitch choice. Triadic formations and octave

7 In 'Letter to Lee Hepner,' 95, Somers wrote that in Paris in 1950 he 'explored areas of compositional technique other than the highly organic serialism I had been working on. (Though that was not particularly displayed in my free compositions.)'

2.5 Woodwind Quintet: a/ first movement series; b/ opening chord sequence of first movement (bars 1–3); c/ first part of main melodic line (bars 7–11)

leaps are not avoided. There is little point in analysing the flute melody in terms of the series, yet sketches show that in early stages it was consciously derived from the series. An important scale-like idea in the middle sections of the movement bears no relation to the original series, yet accompaniment figures and melodic ideas in the A' section are derived from small segments of the original series. Thus, treated freely, the series is merely a repository of interval segments which can take on an independent motivic life of their own outside the series itself.[8]

During 1947 and 1948 Somers began to attract wide attention as a performer and composer. Victor Feldbrill, who was a fellow student at the conservatory during those years and subsequently became a close friend and colleague, recalls that the first time he heard Somers play the *Testament of Youth* he was 'completely mesmerized' by both music and performer. There was little of the traditional artist's struggle for recognition in Somers' case; from the beginning there seems to have been a general consensus that he was a major creative figure. The following chronology of those years indicates the major events in his career:

8 The above procedures reflect Weinzweig's belief that serial technique was a useful way to become acquainted with the potential of various intervals.

1947
February: 'Shadows' performed under the Australian conductor Bernard Heinze on the CBC's 'Sunday Night Concert' (later that year performed by Heinze in Melbourne, Australia)
April: half-hour piano recital on CBC radio included *Testament of Youth* and works by Liszt, Chopin, and Debussy
July: Scherzo for Strings broadcast by Harold Sumberg's Symphony for Strings (subsequently performed twice by the Toronto Symphony and recorded for the CBC International Service)
December: performance of Suite for Percussion at the Arts and Letters Club of Toronto
1948
March: Sketches for Orchestra and String Quartet No. 1 performed at International Music Students' Symposium at Eastman School, Rochester
March: Two piano recitals at the Royal Conservatory, one devoted entirely to his own music (Piano Sonata No. 2, *Strangeness of Heart, Étude, Dark and Light, Flights of Fancy*, Three Sonnets) and the other to music by Barbara Pentland
November: CBC 'Wednesday Night' broadcast of the Rhapsody for Violin and Piano, Scherzo for Strings, and *North Country*, the latter two by the CBC String Orchestra under Geoffrey Waddington
1949
May: performance of Piano Concerto No. 1 by the composer and the Royal Conservatory Orchestra, conducted by Ettore Mazzoleni

In 1948, through the interest and special attention of Jean Howson, the first director of the serious music division of BMI Canada Ltd. (the performing-rights and publishing firm), three of Somers' works were published by that firm: *Strangeness of Heart*, Three Sonnets, and *A Bunch of Rowan*. This was followed by the publication of Scherzo for Strings by Associated Music Publishers, New York.

During the summer of 1948, Somers went to San Francisco to study for six weeks with the eminent pianist and pedagogue E. Robert Schmitz (1889–1949), whom he had already met in Toronto. Schmitz exerted a strong influence on Somers' development during the late forties, making him aware, for instance, of the importance of the precise dynamic and other markings in Debussy's music – a precision which found its way into Somers' own scores. At the end of the study session, in a competition concert, he shared third prize with another student. He evidently regarded this as the equivalent of a failure and began to question seriously his dual career as pianist and composer. One notes that *North Country*, one of the two most mature pieces of the period (the other being the Suite for Harp and Chamber Orchestra), was written in the autumn of the same year, following the experience in San Francisco. By 1949 the major portion of his musical drive was being channeled into composition.[9]

The last three large works of the 1940s – Rhapsody for Violin and Piano, *North Country*, and the Suite for Harp and Chamber Orchestra – were the last written under Weinzweig's guidance, and are also the earliest works to be widely known today. While certain characteristics of these works (especially of *North Country*) have come to be identified with Somers' mature style, it must be remembered that these characteristics are present already in earlier works of the forties. It is because they are now used with more assurance and consistency than ever before that one can speak of a Somers style.

Although the Rhapsody for Violin and Piano (written between 26 May and 2 June 1948 and dedicated to the composer's future wife Catherine Mackie) shares certain characteristics with its larger companions, more than a trace of the ample declamatory gestures and impassioned outbursts of earlier works remains in its two *appassionato* sections, with their intense, rhapsodic lines and surging piano chords. the overall structure of the work can be shown as in chart 1 (p. 33). The build-up and release of tension, an important structural device, as the chart shows, is achieved not only by the shape of individual ideas and the juxtaposition of thick, relatively dissonant textures with thinner, more tonally explicit ones, but by the use of dynamic contrast within a section or between sections as a lever to create what the composer later called 'dynamic unrest.' From this point of view, one of the most striking features of the work is the contrast between the quiet, practically unaccompanied violin line in the transition before the return of A', and its return at the end in a high register, at *ff* level, subjected to sharp, isolated chordal interjections in the piano. This basic gesture – a continuous, intense melodic line 'attacked' by sharp isolated fragments – returns in many guises in later works. The interjections seem to articulate another facet of the tension underlying such a melodic line.

9 See Harvey Olnick 'Harry Somers' 8, which cites a letter written by Somers to his mother, in which he questions for the first time the advisability of pursuing a double career.

CHART I
Structural outline of the Rhapsody for Violin and Piano

A	transition 1	B	C	transition 2
first theme (containing the series) introduced imitatively	'long line' in violin (arising from first theme)	(Con fuoco) rhythmic, light	(Appassionato) intense, rhapsodic violin line with B minor tonal centre	violin soliloquy using melody of C section – now D minor tonal centre (relaxation of tension)

p $<$ ff $>$ pp $<$ ffp $<$ fpp $<$ f $<$ ff $>$ p - - - - - - - - - - - -

A′	transition 3	D	C	coda
leaner texture, based on inversion of series	piano alone, using opening rising sixth figure of A section theme	(Allegro vivace) scherzo-like, a counterpart to B section	(Appassionato) first C section transposed major second higher	violin soliloquy from transition 2 now in B minor, with sharp interjections in piano

p $<$ f   p $<$ f p $<$ f $<$ ff -

restless dynamic contrasts

The Rhapsody for Violin and Piano is based on a series imbedded in the main theme of the first section. Example 2.6, taken from the beginning of the piece, indicates not only the manner in which the series is used, but Somers' skill in developing extended, tension-building melodic lines, the important role of the perfect fourth in chord construction, and the suggestion of imitative contrapuntal procedures. As this example shows, the pitches of the series are never presented consecutively straight through from beginning to end. In the violin line, after the twelfth pitch (A♯) is stated in bar eleven, only two or three adjacent pitches are used together (often in reverse order). For instance, it is obvious that the shape of motive *a* (in bar 10), rather than a direct

2.6 Rhapsody for Violin and Piano: series and bars 1–15 (the latter in the composer's hand)

succession of pitches from the series, is the important factor in extending the melodic line, in addition to a stepwise sequence marked x in the example. This figure x (pitches 9, 11, 10, 5, 7 of the series) is used as the basis of the melodic lines in contrasting sections of the piece; its quasitonal implications give these lines considerable intensity and stability. As mentioned above, the tonal implications (D minor) of the violin line in the transition back to A' help to create a sense of dénouement and relaxation.

North Country (subtitled Four Movements for String Orchestra) was written in the fall of 1948. It is the last work to bear a descriptive title, but the title was added after the piece was completed. A discarded, partially completed version of the first movement is entitled Sonata for String Orchestra. Essentially the work is a four-movement suite, with two fast outer movements surrounding the scherzo-like second and slow third movements. Notwithstanding, the music (particularly of the first movement) is highly suggestive of certain qualities one associates with the vast semi-wilderness of northern Ontario – bleakness, ruggedness, and loneliness. The musical characteristics which suggest these qualities are not difficult to isolate: the taut, lean textures and nervous rhythmic vitality (especially of the outer two movements), and the spare, thin melodic lines (especially in a high register, as in the first movement) are the most obvious traits. Mention has already been made of Somers' periodic visits to northern Ontario during the forties – the qualities of that landscape were engrained in his consciousness.

Perhaps another, more subtle evocative quality (and one of the chief characteristics of Somers' music after *North Country*) is the suggestion of unrest and tension underlying a seemingly controlled, calm exterior (which itself has an inner level of tension-building relationships). The most obvious example is the introduction to the first movement, which is a direct counterpart of the coda of the Rhapsody for Violin and Piano. This introduction consists of four asymmetrical melodic units in a high register of the first violins, punctuated by full *sffz* chords which overlap from phrase to phrase (example 2.7). The first violin line is built around a tiny interval cell (marked x), consisting of a perfect fourth surrounded at each end by a second (which may either be major or minor). This cell becomes, in the central part of the movement, the basis of the ostinato-like accompaniment. Each of the first three phrases, rising higher and separated from the preceding one by expanding intervals, contains a tonal centre: A for the first, B for the second, and A again for the third. But none of these phrases resolves on its 'tonic,' with the result that the listener's expectations are left unfulfilled from phrase to phrase. The 'resolution,' when it comes on the A at the beginning of the fourth phrase, adds a new element of surprise by its high range and *pp* dynamic level. The fourth phrase is virtually a summary of all the preceding ones: the opening A–G (marked a) expanded, the cell (x) of the second and third phrases (especially the fourth E–B), and the final note of the third

2.7 *North Country*: first movement, introduction

phrase (c). The underlying chords, with their sharp *sffz* jabs, add a more overt dimension to the subdued tension of the violin line. The chords themselves are constructed largely in fourths and fifths superimposed; the parallel movement of the underlying open fifth, in a circular manner from Eb back to Eb, is a typical kind of chord progression in earlier works of the forties, especially the first movement of the Piano Concerto No. 1 or the first transition of the Rhapsody for Violin and Piano. Further examples of parallel chord movement can be found in the slow movement (for example, thirteenth chords) and fourth movement (more extensively chords in open fifths) of *North Country*.

Example 2.7 shows an additional characteristic of Somers' mature style – the use of the dynamic envelope, applied to a single sustained pitch (whether isolated or part of a longer line), to a complete melodic unit, or to a vertical aggregate of two or more pitches. The first two types may be seen in the fourth and first three phrases respectively of the introduction. In an earlier, less compact version of the introduction, the accompaniment chords are insistently repeated and sustained, with an envelope of *pp* $\underset{}{\longleftarrow}$ *fff*, instead of the *sffz* of the final version.[10] In the central part of the first movement, the dynamic envelope *pp* $\underset{}{\longleftarrow}$ *ff* becomes the basic shape in the overall sense of movement towards a climax. There are three larger sections here:

A

The first violins present an elongated version of the first three phrases of the introduction, as if in slow motion, stretched out to thirty bars, and accompanied by steady ostinato-like eighth-note figures (derived from x) in cellos and violas, and fragmented, irregular figures in the second violins.

A'

While first violins continue with a free extension of the line (using figure x as a basis), the second violins participate in an intertwining dialogue with the firsts, sharing the same material, and eventually indulging briefly in a short canon; the accompaniment of the first thirty bars is repeated underneath.

B

After presenting the third phrase of the introduction transposed, in unison, the upper two lines go separate ways again but the melodic units become shorter until at the climax two-note, falling semitone figures are used almost exclusively; the accompaniment becomes denser during this section (continuing the same figures from before).

In the return of the introduction, the four original phrases are presented in unison by the violins, violas, and cellos, transposed down an octave and a major sixth. The *sffz* chords are missing, and only remnants of them appear at the end, in three isolated staccato jabs. The last sustained pitch is an E♭ – which was the 'root' of the first chord of the introduction.

It is not possible here to give detailed analysis of the other three movements, which are as fascinating to the ear and mind as the first. The second movement (Allegro scherzando) provides attractive light relief from the austerity of the previous movement. It progresses from thin, fragile textures and sounds (rapid pizzicato repeated notes and

---

10 The earlier version thus anticipates works of the late fifties and sixties in which blocks of orchestral sonority, each with its own dynamic envelope, are juxtaposed (*Lyric* or *Stereophony*, for example). Somers has referred to this device as 'dynamic unrest'; see 'Letter to Lee Hepner' 90.

slow glissandi descending into the low register of the cellos), through the imitative presentation of a playful, dance-like figure to a broader, more typical melodic idea presented finally in unison with fragments of earlier ideas. The control of motivic coherence and unity is admirable. Much of the material of this movement and of the slow movement is based on figure x of the first movement. The third movement, by contrast, is largely serene and reflective. The outer sections enclose a more 'atmospheric' middle section – gentle trills and tremolo figures accompanying an imitative restatement of the main melodic idea in violas and cellos. This section in turn is enclosed by brief, agitated interludes of a more fragmentary nature (which in each case settle down again to the quiet, lyrical mood of the whole). Here again, there is the idea of surface tranquility broken temporarily by unrest and tension. Unfortunately, the work as a whole suffers from a lack of balance caused by the brevity of the last movement (only fifty-five seconds as compared to five and one-quarter minutes in the first). Nevertheless, the movement has a terse, driving buoyancy which brings the work to a satisfying conclusion. The texture is very lean (two-part, with doublings) and consists of a highly charged, rhythmically irregular, and fragmented melodic line that features falling minor second figures prominently

and is accompanied by thin chords built in open fifths, moving in irregular rhythms based on $\frac{4}{4}$

(see example 2.8).

In the opinion of this writer, *North Country* remains to the present day one of Somers' most original and striking achievements. It contains all of the important elements of his language during the fifties and sixties: the lean, highly strung melodic lines; thin transparent textures, often involving considerable contrapuntal organization; the tight thematic control; the use of the extended orchestral crescendo as a structural device; the restless dynamic contrasts; and the tension-producing appearance of tonal elements within a non-tonal context.

The Suite for Harp and Chamber Orchestra, written during the late summer of 1949, is a gentler counterpart of *North Country*, sharing the same four-movement scheme of fast–scherzo–slow–fast. It was commis-

2.8 *North Country*: fourth movement, bars 1–4

sioned jointly by BMI Canada Ltd and Edna Phillips, harpist of the
Philadelphia Orchestra, who never performed it, apparently because it
was too 'modern' for her taste. The work finally received its first performance on 11 December 1952 at a Canadian League of Composers concert in Toronto. The suite is one of Somers' most attractive and accessible works and has become well known through recordings and frequent
performances. It was scored for strings and flute, oboe, clarinet, and
bassoon in order to ensure sufficient contrasts of colour, yet enable the
soloist to be clearly heard. The result is a transparent, carefully balanced score, in which the strings and woodwinds provide discreet accompaniment to the soloist but at times play a more forceful role –
interpreting, commenting, or providing dramatic contrasts or interludes, as the case may be.

Before writing the suite, Somers spent a considerable period of time
investigating the Salzedo techniques of producing new harp colours,
with the result that a wide range of sonority is explored: different
methods of playing chords, pedal-change glissandi, harmonics, 'xylo-
phone' articulation, and special muting effects. These are not, however, merely exhibited in the manner of a catalogue but are used with
taste and direction, as part of an over-all musical conception. For
instance, the muting effect in the second movement (each quarter note
of the bass is stopped with the hand immediately, while the upper line is
muted by a cloth woven through the strings) gives the harp a dry,
detached quality very appropriate for parodying the woodwinds. But the
harp writing throughout is largely of a melodic, two-part variety.
Somers sketched out several incomplete versions of the first movement
before arriving at the present one. These show that in the final version
he was mainly concerned with achieving a compact, economical structure, setting out clear, distinctive ideas, and featuring the soloist in a
prominent way. Both earlier versions are rambling and diffuse, and the
soloist is somewhat less prominently featured (the orchestra was appar-

ently to include brass). In one of the versions he was working in a fairly strict serial manner with a four-note series

(which could be regarded as a variant of figure x from *North Country*). In the end he was motivated by 'a desire throughout the work for simplicity and clarity, both in its tonal thematic material, and in its formal structure, in order to mount the harp in as clear a presentation as possible.'[11]

In view of the fact that a detailed analysis of the suite by the composer himself is available, a short synopsis of the work will suffice here. The opening introduction presents several key motives in the woodwinds, over a gradually rising arpeggiated figure in the harp, anchored by an E♭ pedal. After bar 10, the harp assumes the leading role, with rich, full chords constructed in open fourths and fifths, moving in parallel motion, and based melodically on the opening woodwind figures. A new section, based on a new theme, featuring the harp in a melodic role, leads to a short development of both previous sections. The movement ends with a cadenza based on previous material and punctuated at the end by a single sustained chord (actually the harp's anchor chord from bar 11) with a dynamic envelope of *sffz pp* $\prec$ *f* $\succ$ *ppp*. In spite of the tight motivic and harmonic unity (the chord structure is extremely consistent), the movement has a very free, improvised quality which is set up in the tentative arpeggios of the introduction – as if the harp is strumming a few chords, to warm up.

The second movement is one of the few genuinely humorous pieces in Somers' music – a charming, tongue-in-cheek poke at neo-classicism. Somers described the movement as follows:

The second movement is a gentle satire on neo-classicism, that style of writing which attempts to return to Mozart, Gluck, Pergolesi and 'brings them back alive.' Throughout, the woodwinds endeavour to maintain the charm and dignity worthy of the more respectable members of musical society, but the harp refuses to cooperate and play in its traditional role, but instead parodies the dignitaries in an impudent and even vulgar manner – strictly a non-conformist.[12]

This movement is the earliest indication of Somers' preoccupation dur-

11 Harry Somers *Analysis* 2   12 Ibid. 5

ing the fifties with the juxtaposition, within the same work or movement, of tonal and non-tonal styles (henceforth referred to as style
juxtaposition). In the suite, this device is used to create humour rather
than tension (as in various works of the fifties). The incorporation of a
twelve-note series as the basis of thematic material in the third movement shows how well serialism was integrated into his compositional
technique, and at the same time, indicates the flexibility of his approach to the use of the series. This movement is reflective and sombre.
The middle section, accompanied in the strings by seventh chords (derived from the series), leads to a delicate harp cadenza which draws
freely on motives from the first as well as the third movement. In
sections surrounding this, the harp moves in single lines, doubled in
octaves. Frequently the lower part doubles in harmonics. The slow pace
and interludes between the harp's melodic phrases give the movement
an open, timeless quality. By contrast, the finale (based on material of
previous movements) is brilliant and more dramatic, with sweeping
glissandi and thick tone clusters in the harp, and driving, pulsing
rhythms in the orchestra. At the climax, just before the end, the harp
re-enters with its rich, full chords from the introduction to the first
movement. It should be noted here that the tendency to work in circular
forms – i.e., to recall at the end of a work or movement important
material from the beginning – is apparent at every stage in Somers'
writing, from the forties through the Symphony No. 1, Five Concepts for
Orchestra, and Twelve Miniatures, to Louis Riel. Often this kind of
quasi-cyclical structure suggests a sense of wholeness and coherence or
marks the final stage in the unwinding of tension.

In August of 1949, Somers found a patron in the unlikely form of the
Canadian Amateur Hockey Association. This association, not primarily
known for its interest in cultural matters, had set up two scholarships,
each valued at $2,000, for study outside Canada. The award, to be
made in the field of drama, music, or painting, was administered by
the Canada Foundation, a non-governmental cultural organization.
Somers and Milwyn Davies, a drama student from Alberta, were
selected from among sixty-one as, in the words of the foundation, the
'most worthy candidates.'

In the fall of that year, he sailed for Europe with his new bride, the
former Catherine Mackie, a Toronto girl whom he had known since high
school. He had decided to study composition in Paris with Arthur Honegger.

3
Paris 1950

The most important pastimes were conversation, chess, drinking, and people watching, and these took place at one of the numerous cafés and each café was headquarters for different types and nationalities.

One memorable evening, a bunch of composers, myself included, went to a concert of contemporary music at the Théâtre des Champs-Elysées ... The programme this night was to consist of works by Dallapiccola, Stravinsky, Bartók, and a new name to me, Pierre Boulez ...

The concert went well enough, but I could feel excitement building which I could only attribute to the Boulez work, which was to be the last on the programme; a cantata with the composer conducting. When Boulez entered the stage there was great applause from the cheap seats, obviously the students acquainted with him and his music. The performance commenced and after a short while had to be stopped – the singers were completely lost. Some boos and hisses from below, a great shushing from above. A second start, and this time through to the end, after which pandemonium broke loose with the upper half of the house cheering, the lower hissing and booing, and a shouting exchange of insults between both. It was certainly the most exciting response I had witnessed in a concert hall, accustomed as I was to old Toronto and Massey Hall.

After the concert we adjourned to a café and a long and heated discussion. 'Stravinsky and Bartók, that was music!' – 'Boulez is noise!' I finally countered that Boulez's music was an unfamiliar world to me, but that such remarks as theirs were familiar to the history of music.

CBC 'Music of Today' series, 24 January 1968

The author of these reminiscences had come to Paris in the fall of 1949 in the hope of studying privately with Arthur Honegger but finally ended up in the composition class of Darius Milhaud. In Toronto during the late forties he had heard Honegger's *Symphonie liturgique* and no doubt recognized in that brooding, semi-programmatic work a kindred spirit. A few years previously, he had himself editorialized musically about war. Beyond a certain austerity, a starkness shared by both composers (and particularly evident in slow movements of the works Somers wrote that year in Paris), there were common musical traits – the dissonant contrapuntal textures based on baroque rhythms and techniques, the extended melodic line, and the economical development of thematic ideas within traditional structures.

Before leaving Toronto Somers had sent a number of scores to Honegger, confident that he would be accepted as a student, but every time he went to Honegger's studio in the Boulevard de Clichy to arrange for lessons, Honegger was out. Finally, after several frustrating weeks, he impetuously retrieved his manuscripts from a nonplussed Madame Honegger and went immediately to see Darius Milhaud, who agreed to let him join his composition class.[1]

Harry and his wife took a room in a pension in the centre of the Montparnasse-Boulevard Raspail district which during the twenties and thirties had been a mecca for artists and writers – Joyce, Hemingway, Stein, Scott Fitzgerald, Callaghan, and so on. He was constantly amazed by the importance the French attached to artistic endeavours ('I was staggered when I wasn't regarded as somewhat mad for my concern with music').[2] In spite of the material deprivation caused by the war, theatre and music were thriving. And when a rented seven-foot Bechstein grand arrived at his pension, the landlord was startled but respectful. The room was so small that in off hours the piano lid doubled as a dining room table.

For an acquaintance with the more *avant-garde* trends in the musical world of 1950, Somers had to rely on experiences like that recalled at the beginning of this chapter. The name of Messiaen, for example, never came up in Milhaud's class, and twelve-note technique was regarded with suspicion as a system for turning out great quantities of music rather mechanically. But the experience opened his eyes to new areas

---

1 A more detailed account of the Honegger-Milhaud episode, recalled by Somers with characteristic wit, may be found in Such 'Harry Somers' 39–41. Such's account is practically a verbatim transcription of Norma Beecroft's 1972 'Musicscope' documentary.

2 Quoted by Kaspars Dzeguze in 'The composer got started with a grant from the CAHA' *Globe and Mail* Toronto, 25 December 1971, 35

outside of music. Through a Hungarian writer friend he first became acquainted with Joyce and Dostoevski. He was particularly impressed by the enormous themes, humanistic values, and overall structure of *The Brothers Karamazov*. This broadening of horizons indirectly found an outlet in the works he wrote that year, especially the String Quartet No. 2 and the Symphony No. 1, which have greater depth and assurance than anything he had yet produced. The year was not without further public exposure of his music. In July 1950, *La Revue musicale* organized a whole program of Canadian music; included was Somers' Rhapsody for Violin and Piano, as well as music by Violet Archer, Pépin, Pentland, and Papineau-Couture. The performances were recorded and distributed for European broadcast.

The obvious question which arises is how much influence Milhaud exerted on Somers' writing. In a direct sense there was none. The serious works produced in Paris – the Piano Sonatas Nos. 3 and 4 and the String Quartet No. 2 are in the mainstream of his development, carrying on and expanding traits and techniques already present, while the Trio for flute, violin and cello, in a lighter vein, is similar to the Woodwind Quintet of 1948. The period of study with Milhaud seems above all to have enabled Somers to re-examine his own development and musical attitudes, with a somewhat objective yardstick in the form of a composer whose style and attitudes were considerably different from his own. In the end, he was convinced that he was on the right track. But the contact with Milhaud forced him to broaden his horizons, especially with regard to lighter music. In his letter to Lee Hepner, he summarized the period of study with Milhaud:

Darius Milhaud had an influence, not of style, but of perspective. We analysed Mozart a great deal, and I listened attentively to his remarks on orchestration when he was criticising others. I explored areas of compositional technique other than the highly organic serialism I had been working on. (Though that was not particularly displayed in my free compositions.) His happy attitude to what is loosely termed 'light music' and 'popular' music had a certain effect on my thinking.[3]

Of the pieces completed in Paris, only the trio was shown to Milhaud. The latter work was, in fact, written as an exercise for Milhaud, who

3 'Letter to Lee Hepner' 95

had his students write pieces based on the structure and material of specific Mozart piano sonatas. Each of the three movements of the trio is actually a paraphrase of a particular movement from one of three Mozart sonatas. The traditional fast-slow-fast arrangement of movements, the literal repetition of complete sections, the traditional phraseology, and the light textures (with considerable pairing of two instruments, often doubled in thirds or sixths, as accompaniment to a melody instrument) – most of these features are uncharacteristic of works written before or during the year in Paris, except perhaps for the Woodwind Quintet of 1948. And like the Woodwind Quintet, the trio is predominantly a light-hearted work. As a private amusement, Somers based parts of the first movement of the trio on a twelve-note series, 'to see if Milhaud could detect the presence, even in part, of the enemy alien. He didn't.'⁴

The two piano sonatas demonstrate the danger of making blanket generalizations applicable to a particular stage of Somers' development. They contrast considerably in scope, material, and compositional technique. Although both contain four movements, the Sonata No. 3 is a twenty-five minute work of epic proportions and large flamboyant gestures in the outer movements, while the Sonata No. 4 is condensed, intimate, and more reserved. Both works are considerably thinner in texture than the first two sonatas. They are almost entirely linear in approach, but from a different perspective: the Sonata No. 3 reflects (especially in the outer movements) the dry rhythmic energy and harsh vertical sonorities of the Bartók of the twenties, while the Sonata No. 4 suggests above all the influence of Mozart – not only in texture and rhythmic profile of themes, but in over-all balance and poise. Indeed, to a certain extent both sonatas show the influence of classical syntax, with the double exposition and the repetition of entire sections or important ideas (in this respect they are related to the trio). These 'classical' influences are probably a direct result of analysing Mozart's sonatas with Milhaud. In both sonatas quasi-serial techniques are used but with varying degrees of rigidity. In the Sonata No. 3 and the third movement of the Sonata No. 4 shorter segments of the series are used in a motivic way, but in the remaining movements of the Sonata No. 4, the series is applied more systematically than in any previous work. This is particularly true of the first movement; within the first eight bars, the series is exposed three times at the original pitch level. Certain pitches –

4 Memorandum of 6 June 1974 from Harry Somers to this writer

3.1 Piano Sonata No. 4: first movement, bars 1–8 (in the composer's hand)

notably the A – play an important role in articulating sections and providing points of reference (example 3.1).

By contrast, the opening of the Sonata No. 3 focuses on a six-note segment (marked *a* in example 3.2) which also controls the melodic movement of the left-hand chords in bars 10–13, as well as the beginning of the second group's thematic idea. As example 3.2 shows, the structure of the accompaniment chords bears no relation to the series – the favoured intervals are the fourth and fifth, moving by parallel motion. A four-note segment of this series (marked *b* in example 3.2), reordered and transposed, becomes an ostinato bass in the fourth movement.

The slow movements of both sonatas are intensely reflective, and reveal new maturity and depth. At the same time, both indicate the beginnings of Somers' two chief preoccupations of the fifties – fugal techniques and style juxtaposition. The second movement of the Sonata No. 3 consists of two main sections: an introduction, consisting of inert melodic fragments thinly accompanied by major sevenths and minor ninths (as if dangling among high-tension wires) and a faster moving, tightly packed contrapuntal section, consisting of two main melodic ideas which are each treated imitatively before the entire section is repeated in varied form. The imitative texture of this section, as well as the flowing embroidery of a slowly moving melodic line, anticipate the *12 x 12* piano fugues of 1951. Quasi-tonal cadences or areas are used here to resolve tension, to articulate large sections, or to mark the beginning and end of phrases.

The third movement of the Sonata No. 4, on the other hand, is a kind of accompanied monody in ternary form. The first section of the move-

3.2 Piano Sonata No. 3: series and first movement, bars 5–13 (the latter in the composer's hand)

ment shows several important Somers traits: the gradually rising melodic line (with strong tonal components) accompanied at first by dry, nervous rhythmic interjections, then by sustained elements which grow into a minor triad (obscured by the upper voice) (example 3.3). This leads to an intense climax featuring a short falling semitone figure (example 3.4). The ending of the movement – a sustained Eb minor chord with an E♮ in the melody – anticipates exactly the ending of Five Songs for Dark Voice of 1956. The presence of tonal elements obscured by melodic dissonance recalls similar characteristics in works of the early

3.3 Piano Sonata No. 4: third movement, bars 1–11 (in the composer's hand)

forties. John Beckwith has aptly described movements like this as 'personal songs of sadness and perhaps loneliness.'[5]

The best work of the four completed in Paris and, in the opinion of this writer, one of the most impressive works of Somers' entire career is the String Quartet No. 2 (1950). It is a balanced, coherent work, rich and imaginative in ideas, with a final slow movement which contains some of the most profound music that Somers has ever written, although unfortunately it has not received the attention it deserves in recent years.

5 'Composers' 50

3.4 Piano Sonata No. 4: third movement, bars 17–19 (in the composer's hand)

There are five movements, two of which are interludes, providing lighter moods and thinner textures than the other three: first movement, first interlude, masque, second interlude, third movement (there is no break between the first movement and the first interlude). As a whole, the quartet shows the influence of Bartók's Sixth String Quartet (1939), a work which Somers had discovered before leaving Toronto. Like the Bartók, Somers' quartet opens with a pensive viola melody (accompanied, unlike Bartók's) which is the progenitor of much of the motivic material of the first movement. The second movement is the counterpart of the 'Burletta' in Bartók's work, although in Somers the bitter irony is considerably less savage than in the sixth quartet. Both works close with a sad, quiet slow movement. Other details of texture and material suggest a strong influence of Bartók: the short 'points' of imitation ascending or descending through all instruments, square-cut, 'folksy' themes in the masque and second interlude, the exploration of a wide variety of string colours and effects (for example, the pizzicato chord accompaniment in the masque and third movement), and the frequent appearance of the Bartókian chromatic changing note figure (e.g. C–D–C–C♯), and finally, the arch-like arrangement of movements.

Notwithstanding, the String Quartet No. 2 sounds like Somers, not Bartók, and is virtually a new synthesis of every important trait found in earlier works. Surprisingly, the work is not based on a series but is nonetheless tightly organized motivically, using a selective number of intervals – the minor second, perfect fourth, minor third, and tritone (in that order). There are two important factors which contribute to overall cohesiveness: the tonal references, especially to the E minor triad, which becomes a recurring motif through the work (see example 3.5),

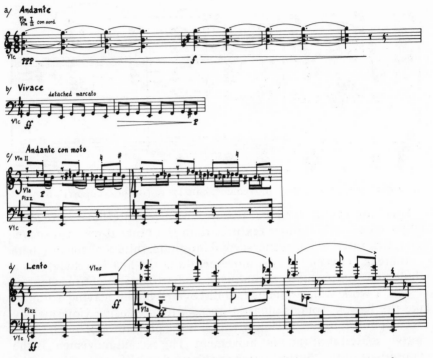

3.5 String Quartet No. 2: a/ first movement, bars 1–5; b/ first movement, bars 41–2; c/ masque, bars 44–5; d/ third movement, bars 53–5

and a falling minor second figure, which appears throughout the first movement and as part of the tremolo figure of the first interlude, but above all, permeates the third movement (see example 3.6).

The first and last sustained sounds of the Quartet – the E minor triad (as in example 3.5a) and the minor second E–F – circumscribe the harmonic polarity of the entire quartet. The recurrence of tonal elements (especially the E minor triad) as stabilizing agents within a non-tonal context points to the appearance of Somers' style juxtaposition of the fifties. In the String Quartet No. 2 these elements serve most often as a temporary means of releasing tension; for example, at the end of the middle section of the first movement where the sudden appearance of a D minor, then an F minor triad, seems to resolve the high-tension dissonance of the previous area, while maintaining a high level of intensity through dynamics and register. On the other hand, the melodic material of the second interlude largely centres around E major

3.6 String Quartet No. 2: third movement: a/ bars 1–5; b/ bars 14–23 (in the composer's hand)

and its subdominant A. Here the use of tonal material helps to establish a quality of delicate grace and whimsy.

Example 3.5a shows the presence of the 'dynamic envelope' applied to sustained sonorities; the final sonority (the E–F semitone) has a similar dynamic contour (adding another dimension to the harmonic polarity mentioned above). The ending of *Stereophony* (1963) is merely a large expansion of the same basic dynamic shape. The device is used as well in the first interlude, applied to single sustained pitches which grow dynamically before bursting into short melodic fragments. Another important technique of the fifties – the use of fugue-related counterpoint – plays a relatively important role in the quartet, generally with all four voices taking up a thematic idea in succession, in the manner of a fugue exposition. This occurs on three occasions in the first movement and in the B section of the second interlude.

The last movement begins bleakly, with the falling minor-second figure forming an additional minor second with its accompaniment (example 3.6a). The silent gaps between these fragments are an essential part of the dramatic tension. After several brief but eloquent cello soliloquies, the movement continues with a tender lullaby-like figure (example 3.6b) which accompanies the main melodic idea of the movement (note the importance of the minor second and perfect fourth). Subsequently the movement rises to several passionate outbursts (involving the falling minor-second figure), in each case followed by the cello's strummed E minor triad – again here a tension-releasing device. The movement ends as it began, with the bleak minor-second figure.

Although the Symphony No. 1 was not completed until the spring of 1951, the main ideas (the 'thematic core') were sketched out in Paris, and the work is really a product of the Paris experience.

I believe the temperament of the work is strongly romantic, that is to say, emotive and dramatic. Subjectively I was responding strongly to literature at that time – the brilliant technical control of Joyce's *Ulysses*, and the profound humanism of Dostoevsky, both of whom I was introduced to in Paris. Perhaps a late date to come across such giants of literature, but perhaps a deeper experience because of that.[6]

The symphony was first performed over the CBC radio network on 27 April 1953 by the CBC Symphony Orchestra under the direction of Victor Feldbrill, who preceded it with Mozart. This was an appropriate choice, in view of Somers' contact with Mozart sonatas during the year in Paris. In program notes Feldbrill remarked that the symphony 'has the same directness and economy of means as Mozart, with no superfluous orchestration or padding.'[7] 'Economy of means' suggests a degree of compositional control such that certain distinctive, compact ideas generate an extended musical structure, without recourse to additional material

6 Somers' program notes on BMI Canada edition of the Symphony No. 1 (n.d.)
7 *CBC Times* 26 April–2 May 1953, 3

3.7 Symphony No. 1: prologue, bars 6–17

beyond the orbit of those ideas. Within the twenty-five minutes of the symphony, ideas are concisely exposed and developed with a sense of timing and logic made all the more effective by Somers' flair for dramatic contrast, and, above all, his capacity to build convincing climaxes and create suspense at the appropriate moment. Thus, the important elements of symphonic writing, at least in the twentieth century, are present in this work: distinctive thematic ideas, capable of further growth and manipulation, and extended, logically developed structure, effectively reinforced by a sense of on-going dramatic import.

Chart 2 (pp. 54–5) gives an outline of the structure of the symphony, together with the main thematic ideas. The work is based on a series (P1) from which a second series (P2) is derived by taking every other pitch. This second series governs the material of the third subject. The serial organization of pitches is far more rigorous than in any previous work (except parts of the Piano Sonata No. 4) but, as previously, the series is applied principally to linear successions. The opening, rising 'motto' idea is an exception to this. The strongest influence in the work is probably that of Weinzweig, most noticeably in the second subject, with its dry wit and rhythmic vitality, but also in the manner in which a few pitches of the series are repeated several times, each time with a new rhythmic contour, before moving on (see D3 in the structural outline).

Certain key elements of Somers' mature language can be identified in the symphony. The extended melodic line, evident at every stage of his mature output, is present in two main guises: one, slowly moving, sometimes in a high register, often with light, nervous, rhythmic accompaniment (for example, towards the end of the development, bars 220–36), the other more active, with considerable built-in tension (for example, abrupt leaps, discontinuity, strong sense of climax). An example of the latter is the violin theme in the prologue (example 3.7). A

CHART 2

Structural outline of Symphony No. 1 (1951)

PROLOGUE	FIRST SUBJECT	SECOND SUBJECT
Lento (♩ = 44)	Lento (♩ = 44)	Allegretto scherzando (♩ = 120)
21 bars (2′)	58 bars (5′ 16″)	123 bars (4′)
Strings only	Strings only	Woodwinds added

ABA presentation of series and thematic ideas 'M' and S1A:
┌ 'motto' idea (vertical)
– theme in vlns (S1A) (linear) all 4 versions of P1-0
– retrograde of
└'motto' idea (vertical)
	– begins with fragmented dialogue in lower strings using 1-0 and rhythm of S1A
	– entry of vln 1 in bar 12 brings more continuous melodic line
	– grows to two climaxes featuring ♫ rhythm in both and falling semitone in second ♩ (see ex 3.8)
		Subdivided into sections which roughly correspond to Minuet and Trio:
		┌Minuet
		  A (bars 1–14) introduces main idea, S2a
		  B (bars 15–44) further ideas, s2b, c
		  A (bars 45–57)
		  Trio (bars 58–110)
		  – begins with woodwind fugato texture, based on idea s2d hinted at in B section earlier
		  – building to large climax with 'long-line' violin melody
		└Minuet
		  brief recapitulation of A using s2a

	– each climax followed by thinner canonic section – ultimate relaxation in bar 52 on A minor triad – recapitulation of opening fragmented section	

GENERAL DYNAMIC CONTOUR

THIRD SUBJECT

Lento (♩ = 60) → più
mosso (♩ = 76)
100 bars (4' 30")

Three-part introduction to
brass entry, using 'motto'
idea and violin (s3a)
melody, both based on
new permutation of series
(P2)
┌ *bars 1–6*
│ – 'motto' idea (based
│ on figure *y* of s3a)
│ *bars 7–42*
│ – duets among strings
│ (using s3a)
│ *bars 43–61*
│ – 'motto' idea gradu-
│ ally speeded up, instru-
│ ments added, including
│ brass for the first time;
│ – accompanied by high
│ single line, slowly mov-
│ ing, in the first vlns
│ *bars 62–83*
│ – explodes into nervous
│ fragmented melodic
│ line, accompanied by
│ sharp jabs;
│ – grows into more con-
│ tinuous melodic state-
│ ment by tutti (3-part)
└ *bars 84–100*
  – brief recapitulation of
  'motto' idea and s3a

DEVELOPMENT

Lento (♩ = 46) → allegro
(♩ = 144)
30 bars (2') and 255 bars
(7')

Lento
– percussion added (tim-
pani, bass drum, sus-
pended cymbal)
– dramatic build-up of
tension using falling seventh
ostinato (from s2c) and
new figure D1:

– all brass and strings
added
– at bar 21 return of s1a as
continuous line in violins,
accompanied by counter-
melody s3a and ostinato
figures

Allegro
– at first light texture,
strings only (pizz), short
fragments exchanged
– new figure D2:

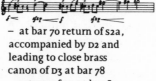

– at bar 50 entry of permutation of s2c (D3):

– at bar 70 return of s2a,
accompanied by D2 and
leading to close brass
canon of D3 at bar 78
– return of D1 at bar 89,
extended, interspersed
with D2

DEVELOPMENT (cont'd)

– return of beginning of
Allegro at bar 115, with
separated chorale-like
phrases in winds
– (bars 150–65) reminis-
cences of Second Subject, B
section of Minuet, fol-
lowed at bar 167 by
lengthy fugato section
based on s2d
– last section (bars
200–85) accompanied by
'broken' rhythmic frag-
ments of Allegro section
– builds long, flowing
lines, moving from strings
to brass, then back to
strings (often canonic
dialogue)
– important climaxes at
bar 215 and bar 275

EPILOGUE

Lento (♩ = 44)
22 bars (2')
– exact recapitulation of
outer sections of Prologue
– inner part is retrograde
(by a solo violin) of violin
theme from Prologue; gen-
eral rhythmic shape is
suggested

3.8 Symphony No. 1: first subject, bars 38–40

melodic climax is often characterized by one or both of two traits: a rapid repeated note, sometimes with accelerando (for example, 76–7 of the third subject), and a falling semitone figure (strong–weak) (example 3.8). Contrapuntal techniques, used extensively throughout the fifties, play an important role in developing intense but transparent polyphonic textures. Canonic writing appears in 'long line' sections, involving two- to four-voice textures (as in the second subject) and in later sections of the development. Fugal techniques are used most extensively in the development section (from bar 167) and are considerably extended beyond the exposition stage by episodes and further entries.

Structural procedures are governed by two main factors: a broad ABA' design (the epilogue is a varied repetition of the prologue), and the build-up and release of tension over a wide arc within main sections (culminating in the most relentless, powerful climax of the work during the development section). Somers' tendency to work with circular forms has been noted earlier. As the structural outline shows, each section of the work builds up to one or more climaxes through a crescendo involving changes of texture and additional orchestral weight. The ability to create suspense should also be noted, especially the manner in which the brass choir is introduced in the third subject. Tonal implications and references are especially prominent in the second subject, where, for example, a quasi-tonal cadence in B major at bar 50 is followed by one in Bb at bar 57. These serve as points of punctuation, adding a traditional flavour to the scherzo-like second subject. Another example is the F minor triad outlined in the series (P2–0) which generates the third subject – the violin line arising from this (at bar 7) has a sad, wistful quality. Tonal references are also used to relax tension.

A favourite orchestral device, found in many later works, is the gradual introduction of orchestral choirs one by one, so that each new colour appears in conjunction with the entry of a major new thematic idea. In this case, the order is strings, then woodwinds, and finally brass and percussion. In tutti sections there are traditional doublings, in textures which contain only three or, at the most, four real voices. Frequent doubling among violins, trumpets, and high woodwinds gives a rich, penetrating edge to melodic lines. Another favourite device is the exchanging of fragments between different sections (especially woodwinds and strings). The use of brass instruments is especially effective in this and later orchestral works; often they are used to give a strident, assertive quality to a passage, particularly towards the climax of the movement. But orchestral texture is always transparent and variegated.

The symphony is one of the milestones in Somers' writing, gathering many strands of his earlier work, and containing the characteristic elements of his music of the 1950s. The Canadian Amateur Hockey Association received good value for its money.

4
Consolidation, recognition 1951-9

During the early fifties I was very involved with contrapuntal technique, at-
tempting to unify conceptions of the Baroque and earlier, which appealed to me
enormously, with the high tensioned elements of our own time.[1]

Returning to Toronto in the autumn of 1950, Somers was faced with a
difficult financial problem: how to support himself and his wife, and yet
remain free to compose. The solution was characteristic of the man, and
indicative of the single-mindedness with which he pursued his writing.
Rather than seek full-time employment, he decided to work part-time,
in order to earn just enough to cover living expenses. The rest of the time
would be free for composition. And so, in the summer of 1951, since he
enjoyed driving, he became a taxi-cab driver. Unfortunately his two-
month stint as a cabby was plagued by a series of minor accidents, which
he recalls with amusement and a certain amount of surprise that he
(and Toronto) survived at all. At the time, he was writing *12 x 12*, the
fugues for piano, and, while driving, would be working out various ideas
in his head. This practice was helpful to his writing but not to his
driving, and eventually led to a minor collision outside the now defunct
Ford Hotel. Finally a somewhat more serious encounter with a truck
abruptly ended the incongruous association of Harry Somers with the
Toronto taxi-cab industry.

1 Harry Somers quoted in *Thirty-four Biographies of Canadian Composers* Montreal, CBC
International Service 1964, 93

After this he decided to make practical use of his skill in musical calligraphy, a skill guided by his observation of printed music and nurtured by the pleasure he had always received from drawing. He became a music copyist in the office of David Silverstein – an entrepreneur, concert manager, copyist, and arranger. While less hazardous than taxi-cab driving, copying presented new problems, since he had always ruled everything. The transition to free-hand copying (necessary for speed and facility) was painful and exhausting, but eventually he became proficient enough to work for one twenty-four-hour period, non-stop, each week, earning enough to live on. This arrangement continued throughout the decade, supplemented by an ever-increasing income from commissions. Although commissions do not usually provide enough to live on, they do indicate recognition. During the fifties the commissions steadily increased, beginning modestly enough in 1950 with a light orchestral piece, *The Case of the Wayward Woodwinds*, commissioned by John Adaskin for CBC radio's 'Opportunity Knocks,' and becoming more prestigious and lucrative as the decade progressed: the Stratford Festival (Five Songs for Dark Voice, 1956), the National Ballet of Canada (*The Fisherman and his Soul*, 1956, and *Ballad*, 1958) and the Vancouver International Festival (String Quartet No. 3 1959), to name but a few.

In addition to music copying, Somers became something of a jack of all musical trades during the fifties. After attending a concert by Segovia, he took up the guitar and became proficient enough on the instrument to play background music in radio programs. In 1960 he performed in costume on stage at the Stratford Festival in a production of *A Midsummer Night's Dream* for which he himself had written the music. He even became a specialist on the theremin, an electronic instrument which produces appropriately weird and ghostly sound effects for tales of horror.

If the decade of the forties was one of apprenticeship, of acquiring craft, that of the fifties was one of consolidation and further development of serial techniques, contrapuntal devices, and large-scale structures in which the build-up and release of tension, by various means, became the most important form-giving factor. All of these elements were present in works of the later forties. But Somers' writing during the fifties also contained a somewhat more experimental component, namely that of style juxtaposition. As already pointed out, the seeds of this direction were present during the late forties in the presence of tonal (triadic)

4.1 *12 x 12*: fugue I, bars 1–2

4.2 *12 x 12*: fugue VI, bars 1–2

4.3 *12 x 12*: fugue VII, bars 1–2

references within a non-tonal context (as in the String Quartet No. 2), and more specifically, in the second movement of the Suite for Harp and Chamber Orchestra. During the fifties he explored virtually every genre, from chamber opera to television operetta, from music for television and film to choral music and solo song, from virtuoso orchestral writing to intimate chamber music for solo guitar or woodwind quintet. Yet, despite the amazing diversity, several distinct threads of continuity can be distinguished throughout the decade.

To begin with, out of fourteen large-scale instrumental and vocal works written from 1951 to 1959, ten involve fugal writing to some degree. It will be recalled that the earliest Somers fugue was written in 1947 (the 'Fughetta' for four tom-toms in the Suite for Percussion) and that there are imitative contrapuntal textures in various works of the late forties and early fifties – the Rhapsody for Violin and Piano, the Piano Sonata No. 3, the String Quartet No. 2, and the Symphony No. 1, for example. Some of these amount to little more than a fugue exposition or 'incidental' fugue (i.e. a fugato section within a larger context). The first complete, independent fugues were the set of *12 x 12* for piano, written in 1951.

As well as being pure, abstract studies in line, these fugues are also among the strictest serial pieces Somers has written. Each fugue begins a semitone higher than the previous one and is based on a different series.

The subjects, which often do not include all twelve pitches of the series, are highly contrasting in character and profile, as are the fugues as a whole. Some, like I (example 4.1), are vigorous and flowing, with continuous sixteenth-note motion throughout. Others are slower moving: for instance, III (for two voices) has a pastoral tranquility, while others like VI, VIII, and X are more intense and even austere (X). Some of the slower subjects are especially beautiful, with pregnant silences or expressive interval shapes, as in VI (example 4.2). The liveliest fugue and from the performer's viewpoint the most enjoyable to play, with its vivacious rhythmic contrasts and exchanges, tongue-in-cheek unisons, and octave leaps, is VII (example 4.3). As far as fugal procedures and formal structure are concerned, generalizations would not do justice to the diversity and flexibility in the pieces. The usual contrapuntal devices are used with skill and taste: canonic episodes (for example I, bars 7–9 or VII, bars 4–6), stretto (II, bars 30–2; VI, bars 30–1), invertible counterpoint (I, bars 21–4), augmentation (IV, bars 23–5, VIII, bottom voice, bars 8–16), and so on. The pitch of subject entries is controlled almost exclusively by the series of that particular fugue. In VI, for example, there are twelve entries of the subject (including the exposition); each successive entry begins on the next pitch of the P–O form of the series. The same procedure is used in the fugue in the Passacaglia and Fugue for Orchestra of 1954. The frequency with which a subject reappears after the exposition and the degree to which it maintains its rhythmic shape vary greatly. In some fugues, the original identity of the subject becomes blurred through rhythmic transformations and the addition of faster moving parts, yet the use of the series ensures that its reappearance will at least be recognized through constant interval relationships.

Beyond the technicalities of writing a fugue, several additional factors should be noted. The most significant form-giving device is the accumulation and release of tension, occurring several times in the course of a fugue. This does not necessarily depend upon the presence of the subject itself, but rather on the evolution of new subsidiary figures which coalesce into continuous lines at points of higher tension. Each fugue, then, is an on-going process of formation and re-formation, not a rigid scheme. In VI, for instance, a brief accompanying figure in bar 10

♭♪ ♭

becomes contracted to

♪♪♪

and forms the basis of the complete middle section of the fugue (which is

4.4 *12 X 12*: fugue VI, bars 13–19 (in the composer's hand)

basically a ternary form) (example 4.4). Relief from sections of denser polyphony is often achieved by thinning the number of voices, utilizing short rhythmic fragments exchanged between parts or hands, or moving into quasi-tonal areas. The latter may be seen in example 4.4, where a G minor area dissolves into octaves after a brief canon between the outer voices in bars 19–20. Such quasi-tonal areas sometimes require considerable engineering in terms of the series. In IX, an A major area appears in bars 22–5, prepared by RI-2, a form of the series which terminates with C♯ and A. The P-5 form of the series is used together with pitches 5, 6, 7, 8 of P-0 (example 4.5). Quasi-tonal areas are generally the least convincing aspects of the fugues – for example, the sudden appearance of an F♯ major triad towards the end of I seems arbitrary and inappropriate. Unfortunately a few places require a pianist who can comfortably stretch a tenth in both hands simultaneously – on the whole, the *12 X 12* fugues are not as pianistic as the piano sonatas. But the clear textures, vitality, and attractive material of these pieces make them well worth studying.

The most ambitious treatment of fugue may be found in the Passacag-

4.5 *12 X 12*: fugue IX, bars 20–5 (in the composer's hand)

lia and Fugue for Orchestra of 1954, one of Somers' best-known and most
frequently performed works. The piece originated from his contact with
a group of Toronto jazz musicians, known vaguely as 'The Rehearsal
Band,' who met regularly in the early fifties to try out new ideas.[2] Somers
recalls that he was attracted by the improvisatory freedom and emotional drive of jazz. One surmises that jazz represented an opposite pole
to the highly intellectualized control which he exerted over the strong
emotional sensitivities underlying his own musical personality. Since
the jazz musicians at the time were also keenly interested in polyphony,
he decided to write something for them in his own style and have them
experiment with various ways of playing it. At the instigation of the CBC
producer Terence Gibbs, who was looking for new works for the recently
formed CBC Symphony Orchestra, Somers moulded the ideas on which he
was working into the Passacaglia and Fugue.[3]

Although they are played together as a single work (actually con-
nected by the final G of the passacaglia bass, held over as a pedal note
beneath the first appearance of the fugue subject), the passacaglia and
the fugue are highly contrasted in character, musical materials, and
balance of structure. Whereas the passacaglia is primarily lyrical, with
many tonal implications, the fugue is terse, full of nervous energy, and

2 Somers describes the origins of the work in 'Letter to Lee Hepner' 93
3 For a detailed analysis of the work, see Lee Hepner's PH D dissertation 'An Analytical
Study of Selected Canadian Orchestral Compositions at the Mid-Twentieth Century'
(New York University 1971), chapter 7.

4.6 Passacaglia and Fugue for Orchestra: a/ passacaglia, bars 1–5; b/ typical baroque chaconne bass pattern

4.7 Passacaglia and Fugue for Orchestra: a/ pitch material for secondary lines in the passacaglia; b/ fifth and sixth repetitions of T

atonal. However, both exhibit a contrapuntal and cumulative build-up to an important climax (although this occurs at a different structural point in each). The passacaglia is built around and over a six-note, descending bass line (example 4.6a), henceforth referred to as T, which gravitates to a G tonal centre (actually transposed Aeolian mode) and bears striking resemblance to that type of baroque ground bass which consists of a sequence of fourths and a cadence (example 4.6b).

There are fourteen repetitions of T, including several variants as well as an extended contrapuntal treatment in the eleventh repetition, during which T migrates into middle and high registers in brass and strings respectively. After the eighth, ninth, tenth and thirteenth repetitions of T, there are interludes filled in with material derived from subsidiary lines which accompany the early statements of T. These subsidiary lines tend to become more active when T slows down on its sustained G, thus compensating for its progressive loss of energy.

The subsidiary line arising in the woodwinds and growing to a peak during the third to sixth repetitions of T generates most of the passacaglia's secondary material. At its first appearance (over the third and fourth repetitions of T) it is based exclusively on the six pitches of the chromatic scale left over from the passacaglia theme (example 4.7a). It is subsequently transferred to the violins and developed (over the fifth and sixth repetitions of T) into a sustained lyrical line of considerable intensity. Example 4.7b shows the economy with which several basic cells are extended into a line which has a new profile. It also shows the care which is bestowed upon vertical relationships at important structural points: high tensioned intervals, like the G♯ – G♮ clash between bass and melody in the ninth bar of this example, are reserved for melodic peaks. At the end, tension is resolved by returning to the line's initial A♯ (now B♭), making a quasi-tonal cadence in G minor. This occurs again after the modified return of this melodic line following the contrapuntal build-up of T. The structural importance of B♭ is not to be underestimated. As well as beginning and ending many phrases, it appears, for instance, at the peak of a melodic line just before the contrapuntal build-up, and resolves into a quasi-tonal cadence in F minor. When the fugue subject enters, on E♭, over the G pedal, it is the absence of the B♭ from the G, in addition to the terseness of the subject, which helps to create dramatic contrast.

The fugue is based on a chromatic twelve-note series which not only controls pitch succession within individual voices (unlike the unordered hexachord B♭ – B♮ – C♯ – F♯ – G♯ – E in the passacaglia) but determines the starting pitch of each entry of the subject. The scheme in chart 3 (pp. 66–7) indicates the general structure of the fugue. Such a scheme cannot, of course, convey the sense of sheer physical excitement generated by the fugue, an excitement due not only to the nature of the subject itself, but to the inexorable drive and momentum created by the final augmented entries of the subject in the brass. Also to be noted is the way in which the focus of attention is shifted away from the original form of the subject during the piece: first to a slower-moving lyrical line in the woodwinds after the second episode (later spun out canonically by the violins), and later to the slowed-down form of the subject. The

CHART 3

General structure of the fugue of Passacaglia and Fugue for Orchestra

I-0

	3 before D	D	3 before E
exposition: entry of subject(s) in violins, violas, celli, then violins, violins I, celli and double basses using P, I, R, RI respectively; counter-subject divided in two parts (CS I)	episode I based on s and CS fragments treated in dialogue fashion among woodwinds and strings	stretto entries of s, moving down through strings	episode II, as before

PITCHES AT
WHICH THE
SUBJECT ENTERS – – – –   Eb Eħ F D – – – – – – – – – – – – F# G Ab Bb – – – – – – – –
(SEE I-0 ABOVE)

	really one extended section	
H	K	L
entry of s in trumpets for first time accompanied by canon of CS II in violins and free extension of CS I	entry of s, in augmentation in trombones; canon continues; CS I in trumpets	dense canonic section; dialogue between various groups

– – – – C# – – – – – – – – – – B – – – – – – – – – – – –

FUGUE SUBJECT

E 3 before H

false entry in
flutes, leading
to set of entries
in woodwinds
over which
develops a new
slowly moving
lyrical line
(CS II)

episode III,
using fragments
from head and
tail of s
exchanged
between
woodwinds
and strings

--- A C -- -- -- -- -- --

M O

return of episode I
and stretto entries,
with complete entry
of s in violins I

final entry (in high range
of trumpets and trombones)
of double augmentation of s;
final note (B♭!) prolonged
with entry of rhythm of head
of s

4.8 Passacaglia and Fugue for Orchestra

presence of two layers of events moving at different speeds is an important Somers trait in evidence since the String Quartet No. 1.

The scoring relies largely on doublings, either within the same choir, as in interludes, or mixing of choirs in tutti sections to provide a rich sound, as John Beckwith has pointed out, not unlike the sumptuous, organ-like mixtures of a Stokowski Bach transcription.[4] An added dimension is given to the opening melodic line of the passacaglia, introduced by the clarinets, by allowing doublings only at certain points along the melody. The doubling woodwinds enter together, drop out gradually, and re-enter again suddenly, in both cases at a different dynamic level than the on-going clarinet voice, so that certain features of the line are highlighted by dynamics, as well as timbre. The use of brass instruments is particularly effective. Figures like that in example 4.8 (in the fugue) reveal the influence of jazz on the work.

A later example of fugal writing, closely related in character to the fugue in the Passacaglia and Fugue for Orchestra, may be found in the last part of the one-movement String Quartet No. 3 of 1959.[5] Beyond surface similarities between the subject material and stringently non-tonal language of both works, an interesting point of comparison is the way in which material contrasting to the main subject develops. In both fugues there was a need to evolve slower-moving, more lyrical lines to provide relief from the relentless, nervous character of the main subjects. Whereas in the earlier fugue the contrasting line grows out of an episode and fades away completely after canonic extension by the violins, in the quartet the new cantabile line takes on the role of a second subject, accompanied immediately by the first, and appears in augmentation near the end of the work. This is, then, a double fugue,

---

4 'Composers' 54

5 Like the String Quartet No. 2, it is a work of considerable intensity and depth. But unlike the second quartet, the third is a non-tonal, serially organized work. The use of 'dynamic unrest,' particularly striking throughout, grows out of the opening cello motive. (See chapter 5, pp. 86–7.)

4.9 a/ String Quartet No. 3: opening cello soliloquy; b/ *The Fool*: scene ii

somewhat more complex thematically than the earlier one, but reminiscent of its concentration and energy.

Nervous and fragmented, the first subject of the quartet is somewhat similar to the fugue subject of the Passacaglia and Fugue. Like the cello soliloquy with which the quartet opens, this subject is borrowed from the 1953 chamber opera *The Fool*, where it accompanies the 'confrontation' (fugally) between King and Fool in scene ii (example 4.9). The 'exposition' of the first subject (s1) comprises only one entrance in each instrument and an extension to the first of several homophonic climaxes, involving the simultaneous reiteration of various rhythmic patterns derived from s1. The sparse texture during the actual exposition (dialogue exchanges of short fragments) gives a gritty, dry buzz of sound reminiscent of *North Country*, together with a feeling of intense concentration caused by the constant repetition (in all parts during the extension) of tiny interval cells compressed into a narrow range, mostly seconds and thirds. The appearance of the second subject (s2), with its sweeping, broad outlines, after the climax referred to above, gives a real feeling of relief and opening out, although s1 (inverted) is still present as a nagging reminder (example 4.10). It will be noted that both subjects use the same series.

In this fugue, as in others, the form-giving element lies in the periodic building-up of intense peaks of excitement, but contrapuntal devices now substitute for the quasi-tonal resolutions of tension found in earlier works of the fifties. The augmented versions of s1 and s2, appearing in

4.10 String Quartet No. 3

cello and viola just before the end, provide a marvellous feeling of slowing down before the agitated, brusque conclusion of the work.

In addition to the works discussed above, complete fugues occur in both violin sonatas, the Piano Sonata No. 5, the Little Suite for String Orchestra (a tonal fugue in the first movement), the choral work *Where Do We Stand, Oh Lord?* (again a tonal fugue), Five Concepts for Orchestra (second Concept, for percussion alone), and in the third movement of the Symphony for Woodwinds, Brass and Percussion. Fugal sections (sometimes only an exposition) may be found in certain larger works – especially those written in 1950 in Paris, in *The Fool* of 1953 (in the interlude between scenes, as well as the example mentioned above), and in the Fantasia for Orchestra (1958). There is no simple explanation for Somers' fascination with fugue during this period. No doubt the strongest factor was the intellectual challenge, the discipline which fugue represented ('I did not want to pursue a direction through lack of accomplishment, because I couldn't do something else').[6] And in a sense, fugue (or at least an organized contrapuntal texture) was a natural development for a composer who was already working with extended line (or lines) and thin, transparent textures. Finally, it is not surprising that a composer who had been striving for the utmost motivic unity and economy of means should turn to fugue, which involves tightly knit thematic processes. But Somers' fugues are certainly not dead relics of the past; their vitality, tension, and coherent structure make them convincing vehicles of expression.

6 'Musicscope' documentary 1972

The other main avenue of exploration during the fifties was style juxtaposition. Somers has written about this aspect of the period:

My aims were at least twofold. One: to achieve maximum tension by this type of superimposition. Tonal and tonal-centre organizations create their 'solar systems' so strongly that, for me, maximum tension is achieved only by fracturing them and joining them with non-tonal material. This, I believe, is not only aesthetic but also psychological, for tonality has such strong associations of order in most people, that it is a shock when it is broken, or challenged in the same composition ... So I was deliberately using memory and association as compositional elements. The second aim was to attempt to realize the superimposition of planes of sound. (The clearest example of this is *The Unanswered Question* of Ives ...).[7]

The device can be seen in the largest works of the decade – *The Fool*, Piano Concerto No. 2, the ballet scores *The Fisherman and his Soul* (1956) and *Ballad* (1958) – as well as in the slow movement of the Violin Sonata No. 1. In all of these, it is used in the sense of the first aim mentioned above, that is, to heighten the dramatic and emotional impact of a given situation by juxtaposing (or mixing) a non-tonal language employing serial methods of pitch organization with a rather synthetic tonal language (often using baroque techniques and forms).

   The earliest example of this technique occurs in *The Fool*, a one-act chamber opera written in 1953 to a libretto by Michael Fram, a Toronto lawyer and poet.[8] During the early fifties the two men explored certain areas of music which Somers had not yet encountered, especially Lieder and Mozart operas, and decided to collaborate. In addition to *The Fool*, Michael Fram wrote the texts for six other works of Somers during the decade, notably a television operetta *The Homeless Ones* (1955) and Five Songs for Dark Voice (1956). Fram has noted that aside from a desire for clarity ('not in the sense of simple-mindedness, rather clear with Empsonian ambiguities'), he was above all concerned that his texts should be suitable for setting to music. It was his intention that the music should add a further dimension to texts which in themselves would not be complete and self-sufficient.[9]

7 Somers 'Letter to Lee Hepner' 91
8 The work was given its first stage performance in Toronto in November 1956, under the sponsorship of Canadian Music Associates. It was first broadcast on CBC radio on 14 December 1965.
9 Letter of 3 July 1973 from Michael Fram to this writer

4.11 *The Fool*: bars 1–10

Set in a mediaeval court, *The Fool* has only four characters: the King and the Fool, who symbolize the extremes of authority and impulsive freedom respectively, and the Queen and the Lady-in-Waiting, who illuminate different areas of the relationship between Fool and Court, thus giving a more human, personal perspective to the whole situation, as well as making the figures more sympathetic than might otherwise be the case in an allegory. Michael Fram has outlined the plot as follows:

Scene i
'The Fool', or jester, loved as a son by the King and Queen, as a man by the Lady-in-Waiting, and with a privileged position in the royal household, announces that he intends to launch himself into flight from the castle tower. The only possible motive for what others regard as a suicidal action is the King's request that the Fool be more guarded in speech and restrain himself in the State's interests. The Fool will discuss his motives with no one, but in a soliloquy he reasons that his real motive is not the King's request (although this affords the excuse for his proposed action), but his desire to attain a perfect freedom in flight.

Scene ii
As the appointed time approaches, the King realizes for the first time that the Fool is in earnest and tries to dissuade him. The two quarrel bitterly, the King considering the Fool's idea of freedom under the law as control of the individual leading only to tyranny. They reach an impasse and the King attempts to restrain the Fool physically, but the latter breaks away, runs to the tower, stretches his improvised wings, and leaps to his death. In the concluding ensemble, the Queen and her Lady-in-Waiting lament a loved person who committed

4.12 *The Fool*: scene i

suicide under the influence of madness, but the King wonders if what he saw was fall or flight.[10]

The singers are supported by woodwind quartet, string quartet, double bass, and piano. This small ensemble is used with discretion and telling effect, as in the slow canzona-like interlude for strings alone, after the word 'eternity' at the end of scene i.

Those portions of the score written in Somers' own style are based on a twelve-note series first exposed by a solo cello at the beginning of the opera (example 4.11). This brooding line, with its silences and dynamic contrasts, admirably sets the underlying mood of tragedy at the beginning of the opera.[11] It functions as a kind of foil to the light banter between the Queen and Lady-in-Waiting during the first part of the scene, reappearing ominously several times before fading out. The use of the series is more flexible than in any of the works of the same period examined above. The main technique used is the reshuffling of segments to obtain scale-like material with a strong tonal pull (example 4.12).

In scene ii there are two examples of an archaic, tonal style intruding upon the mildly dissonant general musical language of the opera. In the first situation, the Lady-in-Waiting, the Queen, and the King are discussing the Fool's imminent flight from a castle tower. Gradually rising, chant-like repetitions of the words 'Where is my judgement and my strength?' by two of the characters serve as a kind of *idée fixe* – objective,

10 *CBC Times* 11–17 December 1965, 11

11 It should be noted that the same cello line begins the String Quartet No. 3 (1959). It is quoted directly as far as the B in bar 11 of the quartet.

4.13 *The Fool*: scene ii, interlude

yet insistent and suggestive of the rising tension. Around this, the Queen and then the King reveal, in lyrical, tonal singing, their personal feelings about what the Fool has meant to them, and their inability to prevent his suicide. The section culminates in a brief imitative, three-part motet (reminiscent in style of the early eighteenth century). The intellectual control and objectivity of this writing contrast starkly with the ensuing confrontation between the King and the Fool (accompanied by the Somers-style fugato mentioned earlier). In the second case, a lament by the ladies after the death of the Fool, stylized symbols of grief are employed – the falling second (significantly for Somers, a minor second or 'weep'), the minor key, and the throbbing c pedal in the bass (again, a baroque device of affective symbols). As the lament dies away, the King ponders the significance of the affair, his musical language reverting to the twentieth century; the vocal line is based on the work's series, and is reminiscent of the original cello solo (example 4.13).

Although one can understand the reasons for using these disparate elements of style, their effectiveness is a matter of personal taste. For instance, the section built around the words 'Where is my judgement and my strength?' seems to this writer somewhat contrived and lengthy, although the sudden reappearance of a non-tonal style at the beginning of the confrontation scene is appropriately 'jarring' (to use Somers' own word). But stylistic contrasts are not used solely for their tension-producing properties. A less obvious superimposition of styles occurs at the beginning of the opera, where a tiny fanfare-like figure appears in woodwinds, and is gently 'bent' into a twentieth-century shape (at least intervallically) during the dialogue between the Queen and the Lady-in-Waiting. The device is simple and effective, setting the court scene immediately.

In the Piano Concerto No. 2 the mixing of styles plays a far more important role. Not only is there stylistic 'confrontation,' as in *The Fool*, but possibilities for tonal derivations are built directly into the series on which the work is based. The concerto was written between August of 1954 and January of 1956 (an unusually long period of gestation for a Somers work) and first performed in March of 1956 by the CBC Symphony Orchestra, with Reginald Godden as soloist and Victor Feldbrill conducting. In length and scope it approaches Brahmsian proportions. Its four movements last over forty minutes, and the soloist must command a wide variety of approaches and techniques, ranging from the formidable passagework of the outer movements to the brittle interjections or intimate recitative of the third. Despite the difficulty of the solo part, this concerto is no mere virtuoso showpiece, but a genuinely moving and powerful work of stature. It is also one of Somers' most puzzling works, containing many incongruous elements which at times are difficult to reconcile with the aims of the work or the previous development of the composer.

Thematically, all four movements are limited by a kind of 'head motive' built into the main series of the work (example 4.14a). Style juxtaposition plays a less obvious role in the outer movements than in the second or third. The first movement is virtually a series of free variations on the 'head motive,' alternating between assertive, restless statements by the soloist, and powerful orchestral build-ups to which the pianist contributes rapid, intricate passage work. The movement ends with a cadenza in which previous figures are recapitulated and filled out. The last movement is introduced by a sustained A (held over from the previous movement). Its introduction builds to a powerful climax by gradually accumulating instrumental weight and peeling off layers of A to reveal and sustain successive pitches of the original series. The movement proper is swept along by a motoric rhythmic drive which relents only for a brief solo cadenza towards the end. Much of the effectiveness lies in heated exchanges between soloist and strings – each with block chordal masses – against which the brass unconcernedly intone slow-moving, chorale-like phrases.

The second movement consists of a theme and ten variations, preceded by an introduction and rounded off by a finale which culminates in a triple canon by augmentation in the brass (against a steady B minor undulation in the strings). This movement is without doubt the strongest of the four in terms of consistency and general concept (although the criterion of consistency must be located in the work itself). The introduction is one of the most striking ideas in the entire concerto–

4.14 Piano Concerto No. 2: a/ series; b/ first movement; c/ second movement (partial theme); d/ third movement, and second movement of Mozart's Piano Concerto K. 595; e/ fourth movement

a crescendo trill figure introduced by the timpani is thrown back and forth between the piano and various percussion instruments before breaking off suddenly when the pianist introduces the theme (example 4.14c). This build-up enhances the theme's rather sinister flavour. Its short, jerky phrases in transposed Aeolian mode, set in parallel open fifths, give it the character of a latter-day *Dies irae*. This impression is strengthened by the piercing chromatic flourishes which punctuate the end of each phrase of the theme and finally drown it out altogether. In certain variations (built around melodic decorations of the theme) style juxtaposition becomes a compositional factor determining the relationship between solo and orchestra; in the sixth variation, for instance, while the first trombone presents the modal theme, woodwinds and piano exchange fragments of the chromatic flourish. In other variations, these roles are reversed.

In the third movement, style juxtaposition takes on a new dimension. The stark contrast, for instance, between the opening single-line piano melody, (example 4.14d), which Somers said was inspired by Artur Schnabel's recording of the second movement of Mozart's Piano Concerto K 595, and the schizophrenic final chord of the second movement (B minor, with added C♯ and G) is one of those dramatic touches for which Somers has such a flair. Material for the non-tonal sphere of the movement is furnished by a new series which the cellos introduce during the opening piano melody, and which strings and woodwinds develop while the piano calmly continues, now doubling in sixths and modulating to F♯ minor. The most unexpected event is the continuation of this F♯ minor, Vaughan Williams-like passage after a rather harsh interlude (based on dissonant chords derived from the new series). The piano interjections begin with a decoration of the original A major melody but then become more jagged and dissonant, using the new series (example 4.15).

Two letters pertaining to this third movement, written by Somers to Reginald Godden on 29 July and 22 September 1955, are relevant here:

The third movement is right! Went over it both in my mind's ear and on the piano a number of times today. A long period of silence is the bridge between the second and third movements. Allowing sufficient time for the accumulated energy of the second movement to be absorbed into the silence provides a perfect transition into the utter lonely simplicity of the piano.

Today I completed the slow movement of the Concerto. I think it's a beautiful movement, if perhaps a strange one. The piano does not speak too much, but when it does it has something very pertinent to say.

Somers' mention, in the first letter, of silence as a transition between movements is particularly interesting in the light of his comments some years later about the use of silence as 'an inherently dramatic element.'[12]

12 'Letter to Lee Hepner' 90

4.15 Piano Concerto No. 2: third movement

For all its striking features, the concerto remains a puzzling and rather special phenomenon among the works of the fifties. One suspects that for the composer it was an intensely personal experience – a kind of stylistic catharsis. From this perspective, the echoes of Beethoven, Mozart, Bartók, and others become reflections of Harry Somers' own musical personality of that period, refracted through a layer of his own style, as well as vehicles for dramatic contrast and tension.[13]

Style juxtaposition on a smaller scale can be seen in the slow movement of the Violin Sonata No. 1 of 1953. This movement is probably the most straightforward, literal application anywhere of Somers' own description of achieving maximum tension by 'fracturing' tonal systems with non-tonal material. The movement begins in A minor, with a lyrical theme which, by virtue of its rhythmic shape and imitative

13 For further discussion of problematic aspects of the concerto, see Beckwith 'Composers' 52–4, and M. Wilson 'Music Review' in *Canadian Forum* 36 (April 1956), 15–16. In his admirably worded conclusion, Wilson pointed to both the main strength and weakness of the work: 'My total impression was of an extraordinarily refined and intense musical intelligence trying to coerce and coordinate an immense range and variety of musical worlds, whose musical coexistence would certainly be beyond the powers of any political organization.'

treatment throughout, gives the first part of the movement the character of a *ricercare*. At first all voices modulate together (to D minor, then to A minor), but gradually split apart into progressively thicker polytonal layers (violin versus piano, then violin versus piano right hand versus piano left hand), then disintegrate completely into non-tonal, declamatory chordal interjections and scale passages. At the peak of the excitement the violin bravely tries to restore the original A minor tonal sphere but the piano refuses to comply and finishes its contribution to the movement with low chord cluster. The violin finishes alone, with a recapitulation of the opening sad melody (in A minor).

If this movement creates tension by its own internal events, it is equally disturbing, in an inverse way, in the context of the other three movements of the sonata. The second and fourth movements are non-tonal, and serially organized, with extensive use of fugal devices in both cases. The outer parts of the second movement are especially attractive and illustrate the balance and clarity to be achieved by keeping the piano writing very lean; in this, Somers was, he said, influenced by the Mozart violin sonatas. Except for a few short melodic flourishes, these sections are based on a delicate repeated-note figure exchanged, in dialogue fashion, between violin and piano.[14] It is in sections like this one, rather than 'fugal' or stylistically hybrid ones, that the best and most characteristic writing is to be found. The intense introduction to the first movement, for instance, shows that in a 'deeply felt work,' the 'expressive elements' can be 'disciplined, strengthened and developed' by other means than 'contrapuntal techniques' (the words in quotation marks are from Somers' own notes on the sonata). Here, the sense of conflict goes deeper than the terse interruptions by the piano, or the restless dynamic contour of the violin part, both of which are characteristic tension-producing devices for Somers. There are two interval cells consisting of a major and minor second (interpreted here as a major seventh). Each of these generates a particular element of the movement. For instance, the major second cell grows into a sad melodic phrase (suggesting G minor), accompanied by a repeated minor second figure. During the first seven bars (example 4.16) each cell is transferred to the other instrument, but returned to its original position at the

14 In connection with the sonatas, the reader should refer to Somers' own account of his aims, quoted in H.J. Olnick 'Harry Somers.' In program notes specifically for the sonatas, Somers wrote: 'Both are extremely romantic in intent, emotive, essentially thematic in their organization, and classical in their formal construction.'

4.16 Violin Sonata No. 1: first movement, bars 1–7

beginning of the second phrase. At the end of the movement, after a faster-moving, flowing, canonic middle section, the introduction is freely recapitulated. The original falling major second c–B♭ becomes at the end a falling minor second G–F♯, over a sustained minor second E–F in the piano. Thus, tension is achieved by a subtle reshuffling of interval cells, as well as the character of the intervals themselves.[15]

In both ballet scores of the later fifties tonal and non-tonal elements are present, although in different degrees and used for widely different purposes. In neither case is style juxtaposition used for its tension-producing potential, but rather for the purpose of using, where appropriate, a tonal language or form which has clear associations and meaning to the listener. In the 1958 score for *Ballad*, a ballet about frontier life in Alberta, much of the writing is tonal in a Coplandesque way, and shows Somers' versatility in being able to write gutsy, 'folksy' music, with a strong underlying sense of humour. In addition to areas of the score which evoke the rhythms and moods of a country hoe-down, there is a 'blues' section, deftly scored for clarinet, oboe, flute, muted brass, piano (*secco*), and pizzicato bass.

The other earlier ballet score, *The Fisherman and his Soul*, written in the fall of 1956, was also commissioned by the National Ballet of Canada. The choreography was based on a fairy story of the same name by Oscar Wilde, in which a young fisherman gives up his soul (symbolized by his shadow) to win the love of a beautiful mermaid entrapped in his nets. Generally it is a richer score than *Ballad*, and contains some wonderfully evocative music of both a tonal and non-tonal variety. Included in the former category is an expressive, sad passacaglia in E

15 The Violin Sonata No. 2, written in January of 1955 for Jacob Groob, is considerably more compact than the first, but its 'neo-baroque' mannerisms make it, on the whole, less characteristic and convincing than the first.

minor, based on eighteen repetitions of a descending tetrachord. The integration of different musical styles in this score is particularly smooth. For instance, the passacaglia bass is derived from the third to sixth pitches of the series on which the non-tonal parts of the score are based.

No account of the fifties would be complete without mentioning the Five Songs for Dark Voice, commissioned by the Stratford (Ontario) Shakespearean Festival for Maureen Forrester in 1956. The poems, by Michael Fram, are concerned with the inability of the human spirit to encompass the concrete impersonality of the city ('thrust of brick and steel'). This tension is expressed by the contrast between the first and second stanzas, i.e. the expression 'every grief is personal' and the series of commands 'Be perfect and articulate,' 'Look neither to the right or left,' etc. The city commands one not to 'go walking late at night,' yet the later couplet 'At four o'clock, before the dawn/ In the echoing street, there is yourself' suggests that only late at night can the poet accommodate himself to the city.[16] The poem presents a dual perspective: the poet wants to live within the city, yet at the same time to contain the city within himself. In this way the city would become a kind of inner landscape.

The duality of the music itself mirrors the poem's underlying schism: quasi-tonal, lyrical music (in Eb minor) to express human values, and dissonant, terse music with hammering, nervous rhythms to portray the hardness of the city. Structurally the Five Songs form a cyclical unit roughly corresponding to an introduction, exposition, development, recapitulation, and coda. The sombre introduction, which presents one of the main thematic ideas of the work (example 4.17a), acts harmonically as a dominant anacrusis to the entrance of the voice. During the first song, several additional motives are presented (example 4.17b and c), briefly extended, and recapitulated (following the structure of the poem itself). The second song (example 4.17d), harsher, more rhythmic, builds to a climax on 'passionate,' then unwinds to the brief, recitative-like third song. The fourth and fifth songs recapitulate the original mood and key rather than exact thematic content, although there are reminiscences of earlier motives. A new thematic idea for 'At four o'clock, before the dawn' (see example 1.1) acts as a bridge to the final song.

16 This is particularly significant in view of Somers' own fascination with night (see example 1.1).

4.17 Five Songs for Dark Voice

There are many other aspects of this balanced, coherent score that one could mention: the beauty of the voice line, the transparent textures, the many shades of harmonic colour within a broad Eb minor context. One is struck by the influence of Mahler, both in broad design and in many details. The most obvious Mahler influence is the final movement ('Abschied') of *Das Lied von der Erde*. Like that work, Five Songs has an over-all sonata-like structure, though greatly condensed. Beyond that, the shape of melodic lines (example 4.17b) or motives (x in example 4.17a); the lugubrious, dark mood at the beginning, with low pedal notes in harp, piano, and strings; the delicate, chamber music textures, with voice accompanied by thin instrumental lines (for example, violins at figure $\boxed{19}$ of the score) – all of these recall Mahler. On the other hand, the tonal areas recall certain aspects of Somers' music of the forties, especially the use of triads 'obscured' by one or two dissonant added pitches. The final page sums up all the important elements of the score. The falling semitone line F–E (recalling the violin line of example 4.17d) merging into an E♭ minor triad reflects the eventual reconciliation suggested by the end of the poem ('Grant at last encompassing compassion, to hold within me all that is'). Five Songs for Dark Voice remains one of the few earlier works for which Somers himself has an abiding affection.

5

Paris 1960-1 and the orchestral works of the late fifties and early sixties

In 1960 Somers returned to Paris, this time on a Canada Council Senior Arts Fellowship. His aims were threefold: to observe new developments in Europe first hand; to study Gregorian chant; and, of course, to write. To help realize the first objective, he attended concerts of the Domaine musical, founded and conducted by Boulez. He later described this aspect of the second visit to Paris, comparing it with his first, in 1950:

Ten years later I was back in Paris. The city was now choked with the modern manifestation of affluence, the motor car, but the café habit remained unchanged. This time I attended concerts of the Domaine Musical, founded in the 1950s by Boulez ... The programmes consisted entirely of avant-garde music in company with some of the classics of the twentieth century. The capacity audiences' reception to those new works was attentive, enthusiastic, sometimes very amusing, always lively.[1]

In order to pursue his interest in extended line, he spent a short period of time at the Benedictine monastery at Solesmes during the summer of 1961, listening to and absorbing the subtle inflections and contours of plainsong. However, it would be as futile to look for traces of Boulez or Gregorian chant in the works of the early sixties as it would have been to look for the influence of Milhaud in the String Quartet No. 2 or the Symphony No. 1.

Strong indications of change are already present within Somers'

---

1 'Music of Today' 24 January 1968

5.1 Fantasia for Orchestra

music of the late fifties. As always, his development was unstructured and intuitive, yet always circumscribed by an intellectual awareness of the implications and possibilities of every new step. Even in the early sixties when so many composers were caught up in post-Webern serialism, Somers remained independent, absorbing whatever new techniques and ideas were compatible with his own make-up, yet remaining faithful to the important elements of his previous development.

The main thrust of Somers' development in the early sixties was towards the use of texture and sound colour as pure compositional elements, rather than the presentation and manipulation of 'themes' in a traditional sense. This occurred in conjunction with the abandonment of tonal references and implications which played so important a role in many pre-1960 works. These developments can be traced to two main sources, one directly within two of his own works of the late fifties – Fantasia for Orchestra (1958), and the String Quartet No. 3 (1959); the other in external influences which fed back into post-1960 writing.

In the Fantasia for Orchestra, commissioned by the Junior Committee of the Montreal Symphony Orchestra in 1957, there are several suggestions of later developments. The most important of these occurs early in the work, immediately after the second brass fanfare. It consists of a series of block sonorities, each infused with the dynamic envelope of a crescendo, traded back and forth among orchestral choirs (example 5.1). Instances of similar treatment of block sonorities can be found in all of the orchestral works from *Lyric* (1960) up to and including *Stereophony*. The major change in later appearances of the above archetype lies in the structure of the sonorities. In this example they are derived from traditional harmony – ninth, eleventh, thirteenth chords, or else simple triads, superimposed.[2] In later works, explicit tonal refer-

2 There are also instances of quasi-tonal contrapuntal writing (at rehearsal number 29, for instance), or important vertical points of repose, for instance at 3, the E–G# between outer voices (approached by the resolution of an A–E♭ tritone).

ences are avoided. In *Stereophony*, the block sonorities are cluster-like formations (spread out or compressed in register) and reflect the three chromatic tetrachords which determine the work's pitch organization.

The two-fold written out accelerando of the opening brass fanfare in the Fantasia also suggests comparison with *Stereophony*. The later work begins with an accelerando, repeated-note figure exchanged between four trumpets (see example 5.8). Beyond this, the Fantasia is characteristic of other works of the fifties and in some respects could be considered a larger, flashier version of the Passacaglia and Fugue. As in that work, there are two multi-sectional parts: the first is introduced by a fanfare motive which is extended and drawn into a rhapsodic cadenza for violins (in the manner of a Bach organ toccata); the second is an energetic scherzo, introduced fugally, and capped by a grand return of the opening fanfare material. The fanfare section is based melodically on modal scale patterns (from which chords are derived), while the main part of the scherzo is based on a twelve-note series.[3] Another point of comparison between the two works is the way in which longer, slower moving lines develop as a counterpoint to faster-moving, primary motives. For example, in the Fantasia a long, flowing melody in the strings which unfolds against the brass fanfare later becomes the basis of slow-motion contrapuntal interludes between frenetic appearances of the scherzo's 'subject.' In addition to its ample splashes of orchestral colour and rhythmic vitality, the Fantasia again illustrates Somers' flair for dramatic effects. For instance, at the end of the first section, before the scherzo, tremendous suspense is built up with fragments of the fanfare figure exchanged back and forth between strings and brass over a tremolo F. Subsequently, instead of the expected massive outburst, the light, rather whimsical scherzo subject appears.[4]

Other indications of future directions may be found in the String Quartet No. 3, the final section of which has already been discussed. In the first place, there is a conspicuous lack of stabilizing tonal references, not only in the final double fugue (as pointed out earlier) but throughout the work. As a result, once the opening cello solo, with its stabilizing, recurring A's, has been left behind, the work has an arid, biting edge

3 See chapter 4 for a discussion of Passacaglia and Fugue (in which the binary division is described).
4 The influence of Bartók seems particularly strong in the work – for example, the short piccolo solo (based on a leaping perfect fourth) over a sustained string chord, just before the cadenza, recalls a similar passage in Bartók's Concerto for Orchestra (fourth movement, bar 143).

5.2 String Quartet No. 3: a/ basic dynamic shape of first bar of cello soliloquy; b/ expansion of basic dynamic shape

which contrasts sharply with earlier music of the fifties – for instance, the Piano Sonata No. 5 or the Fantasia. This in itself might not be significant (after all, there are no tonal references in the fugue in Passacaglia and Fugue) were it not for the fact that there is also a notable lack of 'themes' and 'thematic development' in the work, especially until the Lento molto (at 17). Instead Somers uses the basic dynamic *shape* of the first bar of the opening cello soliloquy (example 5.2a) as a unifying, 'thematic' element, to be modified and enlarged in any number of ways. (For further discussion of the origins of this cello line, see pp. 72–3.) Both elements of this opening bar are used – the sustained aspect of the attack, as well as the explosive release. The motive is, of course, a variation of figures such as

in Five Songs for Dark Voice or

in the 1947 Suite for Percussion.

In the String Quartet No. 3 and subsequent works, a basic contour is abstracted from a specific thematic context and used as a unifying form-giving element. This procedure is, in fact, the underlying principle behind Five Concepts for Orchestra, each movement of which is based on a certain abstract shape or design. Indeed, there are similar passages in both works: for instance, in the Presto scherzando section of the quartet (after $\boxed{10}$), a line growing out of the opening cello fragment is passed from instrument to instrument, and accompanied by sweeping thirty-second note passages shared by two other instruments. A similar area can be seen in the middle of the third Concept (from $\boxed{4}$ to $\boxed{6}$). In both cases, the listener picks up a sense of over-all movement and shape, rather than thematic content as such – although, to be sure, intervallic coherence is ensured in both cases by the series.

Procedures like these can also be regarded as a direct outgrowth of Somers' earlier trait of superimposing two or more layers of musical events, each defined by an individual characteristic (speed, degree of continuity, differentiation of style). In view of this, it is not surprising that in the early sixties he became interested in the music of Charles Ives. Again however, there is little direct trace of this influence in the actual music, either before 1959, in works involving style juxtaposition, or in the later orchestral works. This is due to the fact that by the late fifties Somers was a mature composer with a strongly defined musical personality, favouring relatively thin textures and self-invented material. The only overt trace of Ives to be found in the early sixties occurs in the first movement of Five Concepts, where isolated fragments, ranging from *p* to *ff*, intrude upon a quietly flowing, independent string line (recalling the basic textural contrast of Ives' *The Unanswered Question*).

Perhaps the most important single factor which contributed to a change of perspective during the early sixties was Somers' involvement, during the winter of 1959–60, in a film commissioned from Christopher Chapman by the giant aluminum producer Alcan. Through the use of visual images and music, with a minimum of narration, the film (entitled *Saguenay*) was intended to depict the transformation of water into a source of power. The film traces the origins of the Saguenay river from drops of melting snow into rivulets and streams, and eventually follows the river itself into Lake St John and through giant turbines, where the power of rushing water is transformed into enormous amounts of electrical energy. The significance of this transformation for the production of aluminum is brought home through dramatic shots of the extraction by electricity of aluminum from bauxite soil.

Somers was stimulated to think in terms of sound colours and textures:

The demands of the film moved me into a much more open direction, and therefore had considerable influence on future directions. Here and there I applied colour for its own sake, considered non-thematic possibilities, and so on. I had over the years considered what I would call totally 'abstract music' ... [Somers then changes this term to 'non-thematic'] but hadn't implemented any of those ideas until the film provoked me to. At least in part.[5]

The use of 'non-thematic' colours and textures can be seen in a variety of contexts throughout the film: contrasting blocks of sonority (i.e. dissonant, vertical structures, sustained and shaped dynamically, as in example 5.1), delicate string tremolo textures, pointillistic dabs of sound à la Webern (using flute, violin harmonics, harp, vibraphone), and massive sustained sonority punctuated by terse rhythms in brass or percussion. In retrospect, the most intriguing aspect of the film was that several specific musical ideas spilled over into three orchestral works of the early sixties, namely *Lyric*, Symphony for Woodwinds, Brass and Percussion, and Five Concepts.

In *Lyric*, the final section (after $\boxed{8}$) consisting of a sustained tremolo in the strings, with percussion punctuation and sustained sonorities in brass and woodwinds (see example 5.5d) was taken literally from *Saguenay*. In the film, this music accompanies a sequence showing the use of electrical power in the electrolite process. The bringing in of power is conveyed visually by scanning great lines of pot-line transformers, and 'intercutting' powerlines and pot-line crust breakers. The rhythmic percussion fragments in the music punctuate the rhythm of the film cutting, as well as the crust breaker itself. In the film version of the music, the brass and woodwind sonorities are not present.

In *Saguenay*, the river itself is portrayed musically by a long string line, intended to convey a sense of the river's expanse. This line appears in a number of guises in the film and became the basis of the final movement of the Symphony for Woodwinds, Brass and Percussion (which Somers referred to as 'the evolution of a motive'). Example 5.3 shows the beginning of the most spun-out version of this theme. It appears in identical form in both film and symphony.

In the film score a delicate fabric of ornament-like fragments (refer-

5 'Letter to Lee Hepner' 95

Allegro

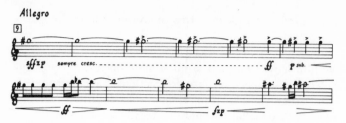

5.3 Symphony for Woodwinds, Brass and Percussion: fourth movement

5.4 *Saguenay*

red to in sketches as 'bird sounds') is used to accompany a scene showing water in the form of a mist hanging over swampy pools and clinging in drops to vegetation (example 5.4). This kind of material, with similar instrumentation, became the basis of the fourth movement of Five Concepts.

In the early sixties Somers began working in the Electronic Music Studio at the University of Toronto. This experience inevitably led to new ideas about sound and texture, particularly as applied to orchestral writing, but he was generally dissatisfied with the results of his work in the electronic medium. The earliest use of electronic material was in *The Gift*, the incidental music for a 1965 television playlet about a Japanese girl from Tokyo who goes on a pilgrimage to Hiroshima. Subsequently electronic sounds were realized for *Crucifixion* and *Louis Riel*, although not all of them were used in the final versions.

In the orchestral scores of the early sixties Somers experimented at first with the new techniques in an abstract context, with no consideration beyond the immediate musical material. After Five Concepts, other factors played a role in the design and realization of the works: visual (*Movement*), spatial (*Stereophony*), or theatrical (*The House of Atreus*). The earliest of these works, *Lyric*, scored for a medium-sized orchestra, is the shortest, most compressed of all, lasting only seven minutes (in comparison to *Stereophony*'s seventeen). This fact, together with *Lyric*'s generally high dynamic level, jagged, fragmented melodic lines, and biting sonorities, gives the impression of a single, intense statement, stretching from the initial violin line to the final

5.5 *Lyric*: a/ opening violin line; b/ fragmentation of opening line (bars 10–15); c/ repeated-note figure (9 bars after ⧈1) ; d/ derivation of pitches from the series (⧈8)

tremolo in cellos and double basses. Example 5.5 shows the main structural elements of *Lyric*, as well as the way in which the series governs melodic lines and vertical sonorities. The material itself is extremely economical: a tense, angular melodic line, first appearing in the strings (example 5.5a), generates several sustained echoes (single notes) (example 5.5b) which in themselves grow into three-note blocks of sonority in a texture reminiscent of example 5.1. Out of this area, in turn, comes an incisive repeated-note figure (example 5.5c). The opening section merges into silence but reappears again in a more compressed form, leading to a middle section in which a new element, a pianissimo string tremolo, is gradually overwhelmed by all three of the earlier elements. At the climax, the dynamically activated, sustained blocks reappear, spread over the entire orchestra, and continue in long waves of attack and decay (with material from the repeated-note figure now in the percussion), while the strings help to maintain the intensity with a seven-note tremolo which dies out only after the disappearance of the other elements (example 5.5d). The final low tremolo in cellos and double basses is all the more effective for providing so stark a contrast with the rather high, shrill sounds in the preceding section.

In *Lyric* there are no themes in a traditional sense, but certain fragments of sound which collide, expand, and coalesce into larger units, always in relation to an underlying conception of building and relaxing intensity. In this and other orchestral works, Somers tends to use the orchestra in blocks, with little mixing of choirs, and traditional doublings (especially between woodwinds and strings) at points of high intensity. As in *Stereophony*, the percussion is reserved for after the main climax. The instrumentation characteristics alone give the work a 'Somers' sound, and the kind of material given to each group re-inforces this impression. For instance, during the build-up to the main climax (at ⑦) the brass group has antiphonally exchanged, repeated sixteenth-note figures (derived from 5.5c). These take on the role of nervous interjections against the fractured, twisted melodic fragments in the strings. Therefore the whole passage is really a version of an older Somers archetype, i.e. the slow-moving melody, with agitated, dry accompaniment.

The next work in this line of development is really Five Concepts for Orchestra, although certain aspects of the new approaches are to be found in the Symphony for Woodwinds, Brass and Percussion (especially in the use again of block sonorities in the first movement). The fact that the symphony is not discussed at length in these pages is not in any way to be construed as a negative value judgment. On the contrary, it is a highly effective, rich score, packed with enough memorable ideas and intriguing sounds and textures to put to shame the vast majority of contemporary 'band' music. There are elements of earlier Somers, as well as those of the sixties – for instance, the fugal development of the third movement, or the long, slowly vacillating, and relatively inert melodic lines of the fourth, with their rapid, ostinato-like accompaniment (see example 5.3). On the other hand, the gentle repeated-note motive of the third movement, echoing among four or five woodwinds each time it appears, clearly foreshadows the identical treatment of a similar figure in the second half of *Stereophony*. The fact that the symphony is an out-going, rather hybrid work and generally quite accessible to a listener not familiar with more *avant-garde* trends of the sixties was a conscious decision on Somers' part: 'In writing the Symphony I had the performing circumstances – instrumentation, the outdoors, and to a certain extent the large and varied audience – in mind. Generally speaking, my intention was to write a work of vigour and strength, and of a rather open and direct nature.'[6]

While the Symphony for Woodwinds, Brass and Percussion is music for a wider audience, the Five Concepts are more likely to appeal to those whose palette is fairly sophisticated and discriminating.[7] His purpose in writing them was to explore various compositional principles and devices with which he had been concerned for some time but which he had not felt capable of realizing. Each movement is based on a particular principle or element, such as dynamically constant 'planes' of sound (No. 1), rhythm (No. 2), traditional ornaments such as mordents and trills (No. 4) and 'dynamic unrest' (No. 5). Furthermore, all except the second are constructed in the general shape of a crescendo-decrescendo (one obvious link with previous works, such as the Symphony No. 1). The most interesting, in terms of Somers' own development, and original, in the sense of the particular 'concept' being explored, are the first and last. These, it will be seen, complement each other: each uses dynamics as a basic compositional device, but from a widely different viewpoint.

In the first movement there is a built-in plane of continuity in the form of a slowly moving line, which grows vertically from the initial single pitch to six-note aggregates, then tapers off at the end to a single pitch again. Along the way it is transferred from strings to woodwinds,

6 Letter to Robert Boudreau, Director of the Pittsburgh Wind Symphony, the group which commissioned the work.

7 Somers is quoted as saying: 'I hope it will open his [the listener's] ears to another way of listening – expand his consciousness and awareness ... I hope he will discover another area of experience and become aware that the music also contains some emotional things' (*The Globe and Mail* Toronto, 24 February 1962).

5.6 Five Concepts for Orchestra: No. 1: pattern of dynamics at the climax of the piece; each new dynamic level coincides with a change of orchestral sonority

then to brass, and finally back to strings, and interrupted several times. Its dynamic level ranges from *p* to *pp*, except at the climax of the movement, where, at its initial pitch A, it returns *ff* and splinters into antiphonal blocks of sonority which, if abstracted into patterns, show a kind of 'counterpoint' of dynamic levels (example 5.6). It will be noted that dynamic patterns form smaller units, and that relaxation of tension is brought about by reducing the frequency of new attacks as well as reducing levels.

The initial part of the quiet, continuous line is off-set by dynamically static but louder fragments which seem to weave in and out of silence from one group to another, and which coalesce at four points in the middle part to form brief 'refrains.' These, because of their greater intensity and louder dynamic level, interrupt the underlying quiet plane of continuity. Each refrain is louder than the last, and the climax of the movement coincides with the longest refrain. Between refrains (which are only three bars apart), a second quiet plane of sound emerges in the form of a sustained progression of intervals. As well as having the only variable dynamics in the movement, each change of interval (or sonority) is set off by staccato punctuations, tripled in all three orchestral sections. Each section has a different 'set' dynamic level (*mf*, *f*, or *ff*). Thus, the secondary plane of sound has a dynamically accentuated pattern of attack and decay to which the primary level provides a static background.[8]

By contrast, the fifth movement (example 5.7) applies the variable dynamic (or 'hairpin' dynamic) to virtually every sustained pitch, vertical aggregate, or phrase. The basic elements of the piece are easily identified: sustained single pitches (which later become four-note blocks) (example 5.7a); a dynamically 'breathing,' sustained note (ex-

---

8 It should be pointed out that all the movements except No. 2 are serially organized. This aspect of the music is obviously of less significance than that of the 'concept' itself. The application of the series is generally systematic, although flexible as to order and repetition.

5.7 Five Concepts for Orchestra: No. 5: a/ bars 1–3; b/ bars 5–8; c/ bars 4–9 after ⬚1⬚

ample 5.7b); and a rhythmic figure which has a long crescendo-decrescendo arc (example 5.7c).

Gradually the texture thickens until, at the climax of the piece, the entire string section has dynamically fluctuating lines, all independent (compounded of that in example 5.7b), and slowly shifting along successive pitches of the series. Against this, in the brass, there are two- or three-note cells, derived from the series and rhythmically activated into recurring particles, colliding and finally solidifying into homophonic rhythmic cells at the climax (these derive from the figures in example 5.7c). The combination of these elements – nervous rhythmic fragments against a continuous, flowing band of sound – is in fact another realization of an archetypal Somers characteristic, encountered as early as the String Quartet No. 1. The use here of dynamic fluctuation, applied to a sustained pitch or sonority, is the ultimate, systematic application of a device which first appeared in sketches for an earlier version of *North Country*. In earlier works, the device could give a figure a restless, fluid quality but in the fifth movement of Five Concepts it produces a brooding, troubled mood, especially during the opaque, intense string passage in the middle. This piece in particular is, for the listener, a moving and deeply satisfying experience – it is not simply a calculated experiment in sound.

Whereas Five Concepts is an autonomous piece of music, both *Movement* and *Stereophony* were to some extent influenced by the performance situation itself – the visual aspect, in the case of

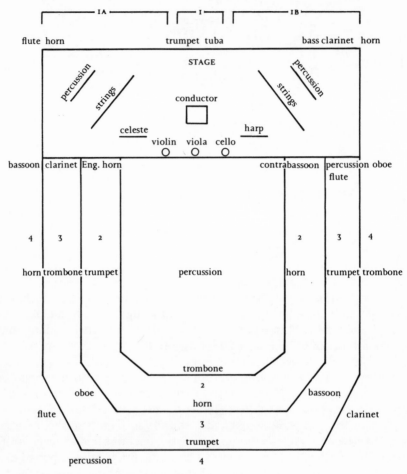

CHART 4a: Instrumental plan for *Stereophony*
4 = 2nd gallery; 3 = balcony; 2 = main floor; 1 = stage gallery (A left, B right)

Movement, and the spatial, in the case of *Stereophony*. *Movement* (originally entitled Abstract for Television) was commissioned for CBC television's 'Sunday Music' series and broadcast on 4 March 1962. The music was composed to a predetermined television scenario of camera movements and lighting, devised by the producer, Paddy Sampson. There are shots of single players, duos and trios, sections, and eventually the full orchestra, in that order, thinning again at the end to a single section (violas). The musical structure therefore reflects this, and

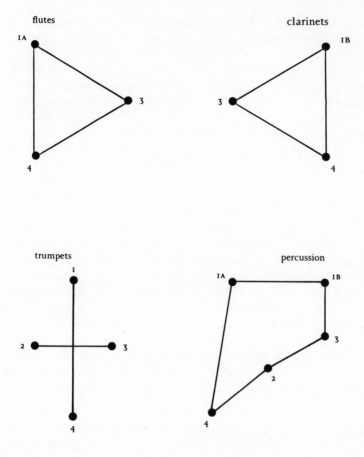

CHART 4b: Instrumental plan for *Stereophony* (continued)

gradually builds from a thin texture of sustained notes and lively duets between pairs, to a characteristically intense climax (by way of a kind of fugal accumulation of movement and weight). The experiment is most effective in working with small groups or single players – for instance at the beginning the visual counterpart of the sustained horn note is a tiny glinting in the centre of the screen, coming into focus on the instrument itself. In the tutti near the end, there was a limit to how adequately the picture could reflect the music. As John Beckwith pointed out in his review, the 'solution might have been standing large groups of players on their ears, or having the picture flicker, rotate, or explode in star-clusters. The music was doing things like that.'[9]

The summit of all the orchestral works of the early sixties and one of Somers' most important achievements is *Stereophony*, commissioned by the Toronto Symphony Orchestra and first performed by that orchestra under Walter Susskind in March of 1963. By distributing orchestral players throughout the hall, Somers intended to make the antiphonal nature of the resulting sound an integral part of the composition. The work was written specifically for performance in Toronto's venerable Massey Hall, with its 'horse-shoe' balcony and gallery, but may in fact be adapted to any type of concert hall as long as the correct circumferential positioning of instruments is maintained.[10] As is shown in chart 4a (p. 96), which was published with the score, no two members of the same instrumental section, for example, trumpets, are placed in the same position on the perimeter of the hall, or face each other directly on the same level. Thus, the spatial patterns formed by members of the particular 'family' (chart 4b) has a vertical dimension not shown on a plane surface. Each area of the hall is assigned a number, so that 'trumpet 2' refers to the trumpet on the main floor rather than the 'second trumpet.'

Another factor resulting from the spatial disposition of players and taken into account in the music itself is the time lag between the production of a sound and its reception by the ear. Somers described the role which this phenomenon played in the work:

Even though the response to the conductor by the musicians will be practically instantaneous throughout the hall because of the speed with which light travels, the hearing time will vary fractions of seconds throughout the hall, depending on where one is seated, because of the comparative slowness with which sound travels, the effect of reflecting surfaces, and the difference between high and low frequencies of vibration. When writing what look like simultaneous sounds on paper, such as the four trumpets together in simple common time in the opening, I actually am anticipating the interesting asymmetry that will result from the time lags and which would be impossible to notate accurately. The impossibility, or least extreme difficulty, of synchronization, is one of the strongest considerations with regard to the nature of the musical materials and their application.[11]

9 *Toronto Daily Star* 10 March 1962
10 Alternative possibilities for different types of halls are given in the score.
11 In his article '*Stereophony* for Orchestra'

5.8 *Stereophony*: a/ opening of piece; b/ 1 bar before ⌐1⌐

5.9 *Stereophony* (in the composer's hand)

This aspect of the work may be seen in the opening 'fanfare' section, in which the important musical material is presented first by trumpets, then by trombones and horns. The antiphonal trumpet calls at the beginning of the section have a pattern of growth reminiscent of many earlier Somers ideas. In the first instance (example 5.8a) the crescendo is coupled with an accelerando on a repeated D; in the second, less static idea (example 5.8b) there is an accelerando-rallentando contour which is the equivalent in tempo of the 'hairpin' dynamics of earlier works. The overlapping of entering voices becomes closer until, before ⌐3⌐, a kind of four-part canon arises (example 5.9). It is here that the listener first becomes aware of the lack of synchronization; his experience of the passage in this respect will vary according to his position in the hall.

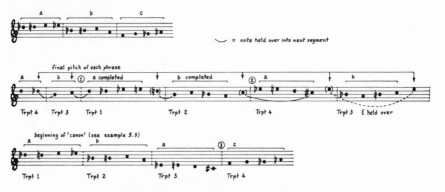

5.10 *Stereophony*: pitch organization at the beginning

5.11

The pitch material of the entire work is based on three four-note series, each of which is a chromatic tetrachord. Since each segment is treated as an unordered series, it is not possible to define one constant twelve-note series for the entire work. Example 5.10 shows the way in which pitch material is introduced. The 'variable speed' contour of the trumpet lines in examples 5.8a and b becomes the most important single thematic element in the work. In the first half of the work (until figure 16), it governs structural divisions as well as figurations in woodwinds and brass. Each 'phrase' in the string orchestras ends with a written-out accelerando, using all or part of the rhythmic patterns in example 5.11. The occurrence of these accelerando punctuations in the two orchestras does not always coincide – at one point there is a kind of rhythmic canon between the two groups. The brass and woodwind figurations share exactly the same rhythmic pattern (example 5.12a) but use it in a retrograde form (example 5.12b), corresponding to a written out rallentando, as well as accelerando-rallentando (example 5.12c).

In the last half of *Stereophony*, elements of both lines in examples 5.8a and b are combined to form a new, repeated-note figure echoed among the woodwinds. This time, rather than being presented in a linear fashion, the different rhythmic units of example 5.12, i.e. triplets, eighth notes, etc., are superimposed at a constant speed in each instrument. These figures gradually increase in number, come together in a

5.12 *Stereophony*: b/ 6 bars after ⑦; c/ 4 bars after ⑦

unison accelerando pattern (as in example 5.11) and break off altogether at ㉙, before the cadenza-like section for percussion, harp,
celeste, vibraphone, and strings. The return of this beautiful, haunting
passage, with a slight rallentando, in each instrument, just before the
end of the work is a masterful stroke (example 5.13).

Thus, it will be seen that the material of the work is based on
elements of variable and constant speeds, superimposed, juxtaposed,
and interacting with each other. This material, then, relates directly to
the spatial disposition of the instruments and the degree to which the
listener hears ideas, widely separated in space, as synchronized or
merely superimposed. The positioning of orchestral sections also has an
effect on the over-all structure of the work. As in other orchestral works,
the various instrumental sections (or sub-sections) tend to be introduced one by one, and treated as separate layers, each with a distinctive
kind of material. In *Stereophony*, this procedure is highly effective,
given the basic premise of the piece. For instance, after the opening brass
fanfare, during which the audience is surrounded on all sides by single-
line, penetrating kinds of sounds, the strings enter suddenly with
cluster-like, sharp fragments in one group, and sustained, quiet
sonorities in the other. Thus, both the sound source and the kind of
material have abruptly shifted. The same applies to the appearance of
the percussion, at the beginning of the second half of the piece. The
general instrumentation plan of the work is shown in chart 5 (p. 103).

Many other broad characteristics of *Stereophony* have been encountered earlier – the tendency to think in simultaneous layers of events,
frequent ABA' or ternary structure of sections, the use of a gradual,

5.13 *Stereophony* (in the composer's hand)

CHART 5
General instrumentation plan of *Stereophony*

I

| 1 | to | 6 |

brass fanfare: 4 trumpets, then tuba,
3 trombones and 2 horns

| 6 | to | 16 |

– long build-up to main climax of the piece
(15 and 16)
– introduction of 2 string orchestras
(working antiphonally against each
other), then woodwinds
– smaller structural divisions largely de-
termined by changes of texture and material within string section

II

brief return of
brass fanfare
material (brass
drops out after
this)

| 17 | to | 23 |

percussion instruments introduced, including harp, celeste,
glockenspiel, vibraphone (really a percussion counter-part
of the opening brass fanfare)

| 23 | to | 29 |

woodwinds (repeated-note
figure), extended melodic lines
for solo violin, viola, and cello

| 29 | to | 33 |

violin sections in both orchestras plus bells, celeste, harp,
vibraphone

| 33 | to end

– brief recapitulation of
repeated-note woodwind
figures
– strings and gongs (dynamic
swelling on sustained sonority)

intense build-up towards a shattering climax as a form-giving element,
the spectacular use of brass instruments, the crescendo-decrescendo on
one sonority at the very end (with four gongs as support), to cite but a
few. In *Stereophony* these characteristics are separated from traditional
concepts of tonality and thematic development and become the major
structural elements. The work is no mere experiment in stereophonic
sound; musically, it is a deeply satisfying work on many levels, and at
the same time, one of the boldest, most original works in the Canadian
orchestral repertoire.

The next orchestral score, *The House of Atreus*, was shaped by theatrical considerations, rather than spatial or visual ones. It was written for the National Ballet of Canada and first performed in the spring of 1964, with choreography by Grant Strate and sets and costumes by the well-known Canadian artist, Harold Town. For this ballet, based on the Agamemnon legend, Somers wrote a powerful, realistic score which concentrated on rhythm and colour to evoke the monumental scope and awesome inevitablility of the events danced out on stage. If the dancers were dismayed by the lack of traditional melody and the difficulty of counting the irregular, pounding rhythms, the critics were divided about the appropriateness of the music. The *Toronto Telegram*'s Ronald Evans believed that Somers' music was the best thing about the production, whereas the Toronto theatre critic Nathan Cohen felt that by concentrating 'chiefly on strident percussion effects and a gliding of strings' Somers had produced a score which had 'no generic relationship' with the choreography. Cohen dismissed the music as 'sound effects punctuation' which had been 'flung together.'[12]

In fact, *The House of Atreus* is one of Somers' best orchestral scores. It is, to a certain extent, a direct descendant of the fifth movement of Five Concepts (which is based on the idea of dynamic fluctuation or 'breathing' applied to a sustained pitch or multi-pitched sonority, and which was described earlier as suggesting a troubled, brooding mood). The entire second scene of *Atreus* is based on this fifth movement, beginning with sustained minor seconds, and swelling out to a dense, sustained band of sound in the strings, with independent dynamic patterns in each separate part. Even the brass fragments come together into identical homophonic patterns at the point of climax. In *Atreus*, however, the area derived from the fifth movement is extended considerably and the string texture doubled by woodwinds and brass. In the third scene there are ornamental elements which recall the fourth movement of *Five Concepts*.[13]

However, another important element in the work is rhythm, and in this respect it reminds one of certain aspects of Stravinsky's *Le Sacre du printemps*. For instance a regular eighth-note chordal ostinato in the strings, irregularly punctuated by strongly dissonant chords in brass and percussion, recalls 'Les Augures printaniers' of *Le Sacre*. A static flute

12 *Toronto Daily Star*, 5 January 1965
13 The opening of the first scene recalls the first movement of *Five Concepts* – a four-part, tremolo line in violins *divisi*, always *pp*, is surrounded by sudden flashes of ideas in other instruments (at a loud dynamic level).

5.14 a/ *The House of Atreus*: scene i, part ii, bars 31–5; b/ *Le Sacre du printemps*

line which appears at the beginning and returns in the second part of the fourth scene recalls a similar trill-like line in 'Action rituelle des an- cêtres' (example 5.14). All this is not to suggest that stylistically *The House of Atreus* is a pastiche of Stravinsky and Somers: the flute line in example 5.14a, for instance, is accompanied by isolated string tremolos, low tone-clusters in the piano (supported by soft tamtam rolls), and quiet trills by a suspended cymbal – all subdued but highly evocative effects, by a composer who excels in the use of colour to set an atmos- phere. There are numerous other examples of striking colour in this work – low, ominous clusters in basses, harsh staccato brass figures, sometimes ending in glissandi, the crisp dialogues between piano, per- cussion and winds, and so on.[14] Unfortunately, *Atreus* has not been performed by the National Ballet since January 1965. A concert perfor- mance of the entire score is long overdue.

14 *Atreus* is based on a twelve-note series which is exploited for vertical material as well as linear. Much of this is derived from the 8th-to-11th pitches of the series:

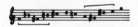

6
New directions: the vocal works of the sixties

By the early sixties Somers had attained an enviable position for a contemporary composer: he was able to earn a living almost entirely by writing music. With the exception of Five Concepts, nearly all of the music written after 1958 was commissioned by a wide variety of organizations and groups, ranging from the National Ballet of Canada (*Ballad*, *The House of Atreus*) to the Toronto Guitar Society (Sonata for Guitar) or the Canadian Broadcasting Corporation (Twelve Miniatures, *Evocations*, and many others). During the sixties he became active as a freelance host and commentator of various CBC radio and television programs involved with serious music. Among these, one of the earliest and most memorable was the two-hour radio documentary 'Igor Stravinsky, Inventor of Music,' prepared as part of the CBC's celebration of Stravinsky's eightieth birthday in 1962. Written and narrated by Somers, the program consisted of excerpts from various works ranging from the early ballets to *A Sermon, a Narrative and a Prayer* (1961), and statements by Stravinsky and those who had collaborated with him – W.H. Auden, Robert Craft, Balanchine, and others.

In November of 1963 Somers participated in the initial stage of the John Adaskin Project. Conceived and realized by the late John Adaskin, then executive secretary of the Canadian Music Centre, the project was intended to create a repertoire of Canadian music in a contemporary idiom for teaching purposes in the schools (and not necessarily fixed pieces for performance purposes). With this in mind, fifteen composers (including Somers) were invited to participate in a week-long seminar in Toronto, which included direct contact with teachers and children in the classroom. As a result of this, the composers were commissioned to write works which would be useful for classroom teaching. Somers' contribution was *Theme for Variations*, a brief sketch for two upper melody instruments with a skeletal harmonic support (which in itself can be separated into three additonal melodic voices). Like other functional music of the fifties and sixties, this piece is diatonic with a modal flavour, and again shows Somers' predilection for voice movement by parallel fourths. Aside from the many possible combinations of instruments (a maximum of five melody voices), the piece may be varied in several ways: by having a solo group go through it first, then repeating it *en masse*, or by having students elaborate the upper two simple melodic lines.

For Somers, however, this brief experience in the classroom was only a foretaste of more extensive involvement in the problems of music education. In 1968–9 he spent a year in the schools of North York, Metropolitan Toronto, as a special consultant. This arrangement was brought about through the auspices of C. Laughton Bird, then music co-ordinator for the Borough of North York in Toronto.[1] Bird was keenly aware of the need to breathe new life into an outdated and rigid system of teaching music in schools, a system which all too often concentrated on the 'product' – mechanical performances of a stale, dreary repertoire of mediocre music – rather than the processes of perceiving and understanding music. As a first step in bringing about a change by introducing twentieth century concepts and materials of music into the classroom, it was agreed that Somers should spend the entire school year examining the classroom situation and exploring new procedures for involving children in the creative process of making music. In Bird's words, the composer was 'to become the teacher, the developer of processes, the explorer of creativity and perception.'[2] Eventually, as a result of this experience, a certain amount of new music suitable for elementary teaching would be provided by the composer (who would also be in a position to recommend changes in the system and to prepare guidelines for other composers).

1 The transcription of an address by Bird to the 1969 Canadian Music Educators' Association convention, in which Bird describes the nature of this arrangement and its objectives, appears in *Musicanada* 19 (May 1969): 5 ff.
2 Ibid 6

At the outset, Somers decided that there would be no point in simply writing more pieces:

I had to get more to the heart of something and I didn't know what it was for sure, but I was bothered because I would see the young people going through their routine and leaving that class and *then* bursting into life. Something was wrong. So I've been very concerned myself recently about how alive, how aware I am in this world and this time. So I was going to use this as a voyage of discovery for myself.[3]

The final sentence here is the key to understanding the significance of this experience, for Somers the composer as well as the music educator. The direction of his own writing during the later sixties – towards a more open-ended, less rigidly predetermined music in which performers would interact with each other *and* react to the material suggested by the composer – in fact provided the raw materials for his work in the classroom and the experiences there fed back into his own music in the early seventies.

A few small and unlikely objects became the tangible link between his own creative work and the classroom – tennis and ping pong balls. In 1968 he wrote a theatre piece, *Improvisation*, in which the performers act and react to each other within a general framework or 'map' of musical events and physical movements. In this piece, the tennis and ping pong balls not only were used as sound-producing objects (bounced on the piano strings) but became an important means of setting up a line of communication between audience and performers: at the beginning of the piece, Somers (who was 'narrator' in the 1968 and 1969 performances) came on stage talking at length about a Wilson tennis ball – his affection for it, its physical properties, and so on. In the classroom the students became involved in a spontaneous examination of the basic elements of music – pitch, duration, intensity, timbre – simply by dropping a tennis ball on the floor and *listening* carefully to the sound. On the other hand, much of what Somers did with the students (as opposed to what he observed) grew directly out of the material they were currently working with.

For instance, in a vocal class of eight-year-olds, the children were mouthing the words 'a crow was sitting in the tree, tra-la, tra-la'.

3 'Composer in the School,' the transcription of an address by Somers relating his experiences in the classroom to the 1969 Convention of the Canadian Music Educators' Association

Instead of mechanically repeating this, they were encouraged by Somers to listen to the sounds of the words:

... I said to the youngsters, 'Did you care for the words? ... There are some interesting sounds in those words.' (I was starting to think about this – the business of analogy– how we comprehend a thing from every direction, and how it is more useful if we do) so I walked away from them and I spoke in the same tone of voice and approached them ... we started a game of imitation, and what was it about? Is the visual thing ... parallel to the diminuendo of sound, or crescendo ... we finally developed a little composition just out of approaching and disappearing, getting dynamic values, comprehending them visually, aurally and every other way until we went back to our singing of the ordinary thing and they seemed at that moment to be fuller of life.[4]

This approach was taken in a variety of situations, whether in a beginning string class or a band class for 'slow-learners' (here he made them aware of their own chaotic sound environment as a first step in organizing some kind of structure out of that chaos). Not surprisingly, the experience of that year in the classrooms helped to put his earlier music in perspective:

... [in former times] I'd write my score out and I would make those musicians obey that set of instructions and that was my army and they were damn well going to execute my orders to perfection, and a good performance was one that did and a bad was one that did not – and so the musicians sit to attention and they obey my instructions and I'm very happy.[5]

The transformation of basic attitudes about the extent of the composer's role in determining a piece of music occurred in two stages over a period of several years during the early and mid-sixties. The first of these has been examined in chapter 5 – the abandonment of traditional tonal and thematic materials in favour of working directly with textures, sounds, and shapes as vehicles for realizing abstract conceptual ideas. The second stage involved a re-examination of many basic elements which he had in the past taken for granted, principal among these being the question of how much should be strictly notated in the score, and to what extent the performer should be left to react to and work with basic materials and suggestions provided by the composer. A powerful

4 Ibid 8   5 Ibid 14

catalyst in his thinking during these years (and in many other composers') was John Cage. But in Somers' case, this process of change occurred simultaneously with another major development – a shift from instrumental to vocal writing.

Until the early sixties Somers had written primarily for instruments. Between 1957 and 1964, for instance, out of a total of twenty-one works, only six are for voice, and of those all except the Twelve Miniatures (1963) are very short choral works – well written, diatonic music of a functional nature, and completely within the framework of traditional vocal technique. Those who had followed his career from the beginning believed him to be an instrumental composer. It was therefore something of a surprise to many (and perhaps himself as well) when his centre of interest shifted during the sixties, not only in the direction of more writing for the voice, but towards a more experimental treatment of its resources. Until then, his exploration of new concepts and techniques had occurred entirely within the instrumental domain.

The evolution of new techniques of vocal writing began in the early sixties with Twelve Miniatures for voice and instrumental trio.[6] Commissioned by the CBC for Rowland and Carol Pack, the work was begun in the early spring of 1962 and began to take shape that summer while the composer and his wife Catherine spent their holiday in the Gaspé area of Quebec, in close proximity to the sea. (The recurring wave-like pattern of the basic cluster in the first song, 'Springtime Sea,' grew directly out of this first-hand encounter with the rhythm of the sea.) The miniatures were completed during the winter of 1962–3. In May 1963 Catherine died; he dedicated the work to her memory.

The text for Twelve Miniatures is drawn from Japanese haiku (selected from An Introduction to Haiku by Harold G. Henderson). Haiku suggest, in a few words, the essence of an emotion or train of thought by presenting the reader with a clearly outlined but incomplete image which he must fill in for himself. Thus, a few short words may be distilled from deep, intense human emotion. No doubt the discipline required to create a parallel kind of 'minimal art' in music appealed to a composer who had, since the late forties, deliberately submitted the strong emotional drive underlying his music to intellectual control (for example, the contrapuntal writing of the fifties).

Somers selected the brief texts for the miniatures from a variety of

---

6 The instrumental parts may be played by flute, cello, and piano, or recorder, viola da gamba, and spinet.

authors ranging from Matsuo Basho (b. 1644) to the present, and arranged them into four groups of three songs each, covering the yearly cycle of the seasons (which in itself symbolizes the human life cycle and makes the work's dedication all the more poignant); this is also symbolized by the opening and closing songs, which are entitled 'Springtime Sea' and 'The River' respectively. If the poems are elusive, so is the music – fragile, transparent, expressive, and concentrated into the smallest amount of material, yet so finely chiselled as to evoke in a few strokes the underlying image of the poem. It will be seen that these characteristics are as applicable to Japanese music in general as to the aesthetics of the poetry itself.

In order to suggest the idea of fixed scales prevalent in Eastern music, Somers assigned an individual pitch cell to each part within a song. Except for the first two and last two songs in the cycle, these cells vary from song to song. Although in a few songs a particular cell is exposed only once (when the part to which it is assigned makes a brief appearance), generally the pitches of a cell unfold a number of times within a given register, not always in a fixed order. With a few exceptions the cells used within each song contain in the aggregate the twelve pitches of the chromatic scale; in certain cases the pitch cell is in fact a complete twelve-note series. As if to compensate for the relatively static treatment of pitches the work is characterized throughout by asymmetrical, elastic rhythms which create a fluid, almost improvisatory sense of the passing of time.

The clearest example of the way in which pitch and rhythm interact may be seen in the first song, 'Springtime Sea,' the opening of which is shown in example 6.1. In this song a gentle swell or recurring wave pattern is suggested by eleven instrumental repetitions of a tiny cluster comprising three fragmentary cells, one in each instrument (bar 1 of example 6.1). Two factors contribute to this impression of swelling and subsiding: first of all, the shape of each cluster suggests inhalation and exhalation of a single breath (not only by dynamics, which would apply only if piano and flute were used); and secondly, each cluster is framed by silence. This is perhaps the clearest example of Somers' own comparison of his use of silence to 'subterranean channels into which the sound disappears and from which it emerges.'[7] Every third cluster is slightly longer in duration and more ornamental. This creates a secondary wave pattern which is further underlined by the appearance of the voice after

7 'Letter to Lee Hepner' 95

6.1 Twelve Miniatures: 'Springtime Sea,' bars 1–7

the first three clusters, the rallentando at the end of the sixth, and the longer duration of the soprano note C on 'long' in the ninth. The eleventh repetition of the cluster (the longest of all, due to the elongation of the cello's B), is followed by a final unaccompanied phrase (on 'undulating') in the soprano, which counterbalances the instrumental introduction. Thus, there are actually twelve events in all (eleven repetitions plus the final soprano phrase) marked off into groups of three; this reflects the subdivision of the entire cycle.

In the twelfth song, the cyclical nature of the group is underlined musically by the fact that the soprano presents a slightly varied version of her part from 'Springtime Sea,' together with the original cello motive. Recorder and spinet exchange pitch cells, in the process replacing the ornamental spinet configuration with echoes of the voice's rhythmic motive:

In this song there is a far greater sense of continuity from unit to unit; the silences are filled in. Other more subtle correspondences exist between songs, the most intriguing of which occur between the second and the eleventh, and the third and the tenth. These reinforce the circular aspect of the group as a whole, and the linking of spring and winter sections lends further significance to the life-cycle arrangement noted earlier (death → rebirth):

1 'Springtime Sea'   2 'Skylark'   3 'The Visitor'   10 'Winter Night'   11 'Loneliness'   12 'The River'

In the second miniature, the skylark's song alone comes down; the bird is gone. In the eleventh, sky and earth are blotted out by falling snowflakes. The second song is built around two pitch cells, the second of which is a semitonal pentatonic scale assigned to the soprano. Her line, composed of three unaccompanied phrases, wafts gently among the five pitches, ascending to the highest, F, once only, on the word 'sky.' Recorder and spinet provide discreet accompaniment before and between phrases (the spinet plays a single rolled chord, at the very end). In the eleventh song, these two cells are combined (with pitch successions intact) into a single twelve-note series, treated by the instruments as a kind of canon at two bars' distance. The accumulation of detached,

6.2 Twelve Miniatures: 'Lament'

light notes in all three parts admirably suggests (to the eye as well as the ear) a thickening mass of falling snowflakes.

The imagery of the third and tenth songs contrasts spring and winter weather: a June shower in the third and a winter storm in the tenth. At the end of each, the moon appears as a constant observer of earth's fickle seasons. Musical correspondences between these songs are less obvious. A clue, however, lies in the appearance of the tritone (a relatively rare interval in this work, which is mostly based on seconds and thirds, both major and minor) in association with the moon, at the end of both songs. In addition to the Gb–C in the third last bar of the voice part (on 'moon') in 'The Visitor,' an A♯–E tritone in cello and spinet in the previous bar appears in recorder and cello at the very end of 'Winter Night.' The fact that this marks the sole appearance of these instruments in the song draws further attention to the appearance of the tritone. Other correspondences may be found in the voice part.

The most complex song, in terms of pitch organization, is the ninth, 'Lament' (this despite the deceptively free-sounding, rhapsodic spinet part). The entire piece is shown in example 6.2. The voice line, composed entirely of minor seconds and thirds (appropriately for a lament) presents a succession of all twelve pitches of the chromatic scale before doubling back, at 'winds' with a free retrograde of the first nine pitches. The climax of the line, F♯ and F♮ on 'wail' 'wind,' respectively, relates in terms of pitch succession to the spinet part, the first two pitches of which are F and Gb. The first twelve pitches of the spinet part are treated freely as a series divided into hexachords which are used separately with pitch succession intact (and retrograded, inverted, etc.), unordered, or else broken down further into three- or four-note cells. The important elements of this series, however, are the first four pitches – F, Gb, Ab, and C; these (especially F and Gb) provide a framework for the entire song. The F, marked with an asterisk in example 6.2, is not only the highest pitch in the spinet part, appearing at the peak of florid, rising passages, but functions as a cadence point, generally in association with an F♯ (marked as a slur in the example). This is especially apparent at the beginning of the telescoped pitch recapitulation at 'wail' (here the two hexachords are superimposed) and, of course, at the end of the piece, where the Ab also appears as a cadential feature. An intriguing detail of this 'pitch' recapitulation is the way in which the pitches of an originally two-part section (beginning with 'd'ring,' marked with an arrow) are later read diagonally to form a single-line texture (beginning with the B after 'pass'). Great care is taken throughout in the disposition of vertical intervals between voice and spinet – these remain almost en-

6.3 *God, The Master of this Scene*: bars 1–5

tirely minor seconds and thirds (again reflecting the F, G♭, A♭ succession).

As stated earlier, Twelve Miniatures marks the beginning of a new stage of Somers' development – a new approach to the treatment of the voice. This is to be found not only in the use of the accented grace note figure (as in 'Springtime Sea'), which occurs in subsequent vocal writing of the sixties, but in the use of non-traditional inflections and timbres to help evoke the image of the text. In 'The Portent' (the fifth song), for instance, the motionless intensity of a hot summer day is suggested by quarter-tone inflections around and between G and A♭ (sung *senza vibrato*); the voice, which never deviates from this static inertia, is accompanied by a pedal B harmonic in the cello. In 'Lament' (example 6.2) the slides help to evoke the appropriate atmosphere, a frequent technique in twentieth-century threnodies (for example, the opening section of Crumb's *Black Angels*). In 'The Scarecrow,' the soprano whispers the entire text in terse, clipped phrases.

Compared to other works for voice written by Somers at about the same time, Twelve Miniatures is experimental and, in this sense, an isolated occurrence. All his other vocal writing of the early sixties is choral music of a functional nature – 'music for use,' as Somers calls it. This includes *The Wonder Song*, a vigorous, light piece commissioned in 1963 by the Canadian Music Centre for use in schools, and the festive *Gloria*, a CBC commission for chorus, two trumpets, and organ. One of the most substantial works in this genre is *God, The Master of this Scene* (example 6.3), commissioned by John Roberts, head of radio music and variety for the CBC English Services Division, in 1962, on the occasion of his wedding. Like the other choral music, it is euphonious and diatonic, drawing on traditional vocal techniques. It is, however, stamped with Somers' personality. In the first place, one notes a preference for the interval of the fourth, for chords built in fourths, and for parallel movement of these (usually by step). Some of the material suggests the influence of Gregorian chant; this is one of the few overt references in Somers' music to a repertoire he greatly admires. The opening phrase in

6.4 Five Songs of the Newfoundland Outports: 'Si J'avais le bateau,' bars 30–6

example 6.3 (implying a Dorian mode) becomes the basis of extended melismas on 'joy' in the second part of the piece. In addition to plain-song influence, several other Somers trademarks can be seen in this example: the parallel fourths between soprano and alto parts, the dovetailing of the upper and lower pairs of voices (where the open fifth enhances the plainsong flavour of the previous phrase), or the tiny crescendo on the final, sustained note of the tenor and bass phrases. Throughout, the text is handled with taste and sensitivity. The choral layout itself demonstrates Somers' attention to the niceties of balanced, clear sonority. The frequent opposition of male and female voices was intended to take advantage of the antiphonal set-up of the cathedral choir at its first performance.

At the end of the sixties another traditionally based choral work appeared – Five Songs of the Newfoundland Outports, for mixed chorus and piano obbligato. These are arrangements of five songs from Kenneth Peacock's 1965 collection Songs of the Newfoundland Outports. In two of the songs, 'Si j'avais le bateau' and 'The Old Mayflower' (both classified as 'comic ditties' in Peacock's collection), use is made of a vocal technique called 'chin' or 'mouth' music, described by Peacock as 'a vocal imitation of instrumental music ... used for dancing when a fiddle or accordion is not handy.'[8] For instance, in 'Si j'avais le bateau' (example 6.4), although the text does not indicate it, the chorus simu-lates trumpet and drums (favourite Somers instruments) as accompan-iment and interlude material to help provide the sense of conviviality one would expect in the midst of a genial drinking crowd. The extension of 'normal' vocal techniques, in this case rooted in actual practice, adds another dimension to Somers' own exploration of new vocal techniques during the late sixties and early seventies.

8 Kenneth Peacock Songs of the Newfoundland Outports volume 1, Ottawa 1965, 61

6.5 'She's Like the Swallow' as sung by Mrs Charlotte Decker, Parson's Pond, August 1959

6.6 Five Songs of the Newfoundland Outports: 'She's Like the Swallow,' bars 9–25

The most outstanding of this group of songs is undoubtedly the hauntingly beautiful 'She's Like the Swallow,' handled by Somers with exquisite taste and sensitivity.[9] (The song on which it is based, in the version by Mrs Charlotte Decker, is shown in example 6.5.)[10] There are seven verses in all, including the title verse at the beginning and at the end. The first verse is set in a straightforward manner, for female voices alone (example 6.6). A comparison of this with the original song will readily show the small melodic changes, as well as the beauty of the two-part

9 Ibid, volume 3, 711
10 The same melody was used by Somers as the basis of a setting for string orchestra in the middle movement of the 1955 work, Little Suite for String Orchestra. Here, there are three presentations of the melody, with introduction and interludes, which, interestingly, use a short *descending* scale figure (which also appears within each main section as a counterpoint).

6.7 'She's Like the Swallow': a/ bars 1–2; b/ bars 19–21

writing (the parallel fifths, combined with the extra-modal B, in bars 6 and 7, for instance). But during interludes between verses, and within the verses themselves, another melodic idea appears, a conjunct tetrachord consisting of tone, semitone, and tone; this idea was probably suggested by the opening four bars of Mrs Decker's version of the melody (example 6.5). It first appears in the piano at the beginning (example 6.7a) and then in the male voices directly after the first verse (example 6.7b). Subsequently, this tetrachord (marked *t* in example 6.7) is associated with the words 'swallow fly so high' (in various permutations) which recur between verses in the manner of a refrain. But in addition, both the words and the melodic idea occur within all the middle verses except the fourth. In the second verse, for instance, while tenors (and for a while basses) sing the original tune, sopranos and altos accompany them in flowing lines using *t* and its words, rising in the sopranos to high melismas twice during the verse. In the third verse, *t* grows into a new tune which carries the words of that verse (in female voices), while bass and tenor punctuate it with short interjections, using only the first two notes of *t* set in parallel fifths (to the words 'swallow fly now'). A texture like this – a flowing melodic line with contrasting sharp interjections – is yet another manifestation of a Somers archetype that stretches back to the slow movement of the Piano Sonata No. 4. The end of the middle verses (which share a common second half) is marked by the appearance of Bb – a foreign intrusion into this 'pandiatonic' music which gives the end of each verse a special poignancy. But the supreme touches of beauty occur towards the end, when the end of the seventh verse lingers over 'away' (again using the secondary melodic idea *t*), then continues into the return of the title verse, now sung in halting fragments alternating between sopranos and altos (the same technique used at the end of the slow movement of Beethoven's *Eroica*). The ending has a bleak, chilling quality, due in part to the clash between B and C as all voices draw out their portions of the scale figure *t* (example 6.8), but also to the lingering over 'away' (which recalls the repetition of 'ewig' at the end of Mahler's *Das Lied von der Erde*). The final chord

6.8 'She's Like the Swallow': bars 193–9

change (example 6.9), concluded with a slow glissando in the sopranos, is all the more effective for being a complete surprise (the Eb has not previously appeared).

From January of 1965 until June of 1969, Somers was host and commentator for the CBC-FM network program 'Music of Today.' Aimed at a general musical audience, the program was intended to inform and stimulate the listener through exposure to contemporary music – especially the 'progressive' music of the fifties and sixties. With the enormous range of tapes and records available through the CBC, every aspect of new music was covered, from international music festivals to electronic music or the latest work of Mayuzumi, Stockhausen, or Garant. In keeping with the non-professional nature of the audience. Somers' commentaries were carefully balanced between the need to inform and the need to arouse interest and curiosity. Although technical jargon was carefully avoided, the presentation was thoughtful and thought-provoking and touched on many general problems of contemporary music, not the least of these being the whole question of audience reaction (or apathy). This reflected Somers' own continuing efforts to break through the 'great radiation-proof wall' which audiences have erected around contemporary music. He maintained, throughout the programs, that the listener must not only reorient himself to a new concept of musical syntax but re-examine traditional notions of the relationship between music and noise,[11] rather than subscribe to the view that the contemporary composer writes only for a select coterie of like-minded individuals whose only wish is to 'inflict all that unnecessary pain and discomfort' on the 'sensitive ear drums' of the public.[12] A difficult new work was often introduced in a peripheral way. A 1968 program of Stockhausen *Klavierstücke* began with an engaging and

11 In a program on 18 February 1966, for instance, he investigated the whole question of the relationship between dissonance, consonance, noise, and music.
12 Program of 21 February 1968

6.9 'She's Like the Swallow': bars 210–15

light-hearted capsule look at the relationship between pianos (the keys are described as 'a row of dentures which … give way like so many loose bicuspids, molars, and canines') and people ('the ones who get in the way of the sound-waves').

Indeed, the scripts of these programs reveal a lighter side of Harry Somers – one which is rarely encountered in his music.[13] In a 1968 program on Luigi Nono, for instance, there are these asides:

In one way or another composers have used their music for propaganda purposes, whether for God, as in Bach, for the preservation of the countryside, as in Beethoven, or for the preservation of the world's great rivers, as in Wagner (though he wasn't concerned about pollution).

'The Forest Is Young and Full of Life' is the title of the first of two works by Nono you will hear tonight. It is not about a young couple playing in the woods as the title might suggest.

Or this excerpt from a program of 15 April, 1966 (part of a seven-week series on Canadian music):

Whenever I'm introduced to my fellow Canadians as 'Harry Somers the composer,' their first reaction is often one of surprise and politely expressed curiosity. 'I didn't know there were any in Canada.' 'I'm not the only one,' I snarl. It always makes me feel like the great bald eagle, or whooping crane, or any other rare and vanishing species of wild life.

But frequently a more introspective, philosophical side of Somers emerges. Shortly after the tragic death of Pierre Mercure in 1966, an entire program was devoted to the music and life of this enormously

13 I am indebted to the producer of these programs, Richard Coulter, of the CBC, for making available to me a large number of these scripts.

imaginative and gifted composer. Somers began his program of 2 March 1966 in the following manner:

Flying on a jetliner at 35,000 feet, I look far below and cannot distinguish a living soul on the ground. I am utterly alone in time and space. I look to the rim of the earth, above, beyond, and into a great wondrous abstraction whose meaning I cannot comprehend. My physical self displaces but an infinitesimal portion of air for a moment. I am a combination of cells passed on from other cells, my entire being just one more cell in myriads receding into the past. The stream pours forth, each cell becomes the inheritor of the previous one.

As though it were inevitable, the jet safely returns to earth. In the absorption with earth I forget the sky. I become involved with daily business. Everything as usual, all ordered, continuing, unchanging, secure. Casually I pick up the daily newspaper as I've done countless times, turning pages, perusing items which I will never remember. Suddenly a shock, an item I will never forget, a name I know. On Saturday, January 29, Canadian composer Pierre Mercure was killed in an automobile accident on a highway in France. He was 38 years old. So simple, so terribly simple – in print. A living cell has been destroyed and I am again utterly alone in time and space – wondering.

In retrospect, a review of Somers' contribution as a broadcaster to this series also reveals some of the areas and problems with which he was concerned as a composer during the middle and later sixties, especially with regard to new vocal writing. For instance, the following excerpt from a program of 10 January 1968, featuring Ligeti's *Nouvelles Aventures* gives a glimpse of *Voiceplay* (1971) as well as *Improvisation* (which was in fact written in the spring of 1968):

For quite a while I've had in the back of my mind the idea of creating a work using singers and instruments (the singers using a text which would be non-semantical), that uses phonetic sounds instead of words, and which would employ the full range of vocal possibilities to create an abstract drama, without plot, but which would evoke in the listener the whole gamut of emotional responses without being specific or delineated.

A new stage in Somers' own evolution of new techniques of voice writing may be seen in two works written respectively in January and February of 1966 – *Crucifixion* and *Evocations* (both CBC commissions). By that time, he was deeply involved with the opera *Louis Riel* and the three works share certain features, not only pertaining to vocal writing, but to broader questions of sound material and musical syntax.

Crucifixion, scored for chorus (subdivided), two solo sopranos, English horn, two trumpets, harp, percussion, and tape, is a short, multi-layered work which was commissioned by CBC television for a special Good Friday program in 1966 featuring the Festival Singers. Visually, the singers were used in a simple, abstract fashion – silhouettes, various groupings, minimal movement, partly around graphics created by a Dutch artist, Anton van Dalen. On the other hand, the atmosphere of the Crucifixion scene is vividly and dramatically evoked by the imaginative use of choral resources. Throughout the first section of the work, part of the chorus yells and jeers, in the manner of an unruly mob, with spoken interjections by single voices.[14] Against this, the rest of the chorus sings (to 'La') strongly rhythmic, chant-like diatonic material. After building to a climax (accompanied by harp, timpani, and sustained seconds high in the trumpets), the entire chorus exhales slowly from high to middle pitch, then spreads out over a dense, widely spaced cluster of sound (at the sentence 'Now from the sixth hour there was darkness over all the land unto the ninth hour'). During the second half, the chorus creates a contrapuntal web of rhythmically spoken text ('I will lift up mine eyes unto the hills ...') accompanied by an expressive English horn solo of angular leaps alternating with dynamically fluctuating sustained notes. Although some non-traditional choral techniques are used – choral 'babbling' and rhythmic speaking, sometimes involving improvisation – the text itself is used intact, and not broken into sound material.

In *Evocations*, on the other hand, the phonetic possibilities of the text become an integral part of the sound material. The work consists of four songs for mezzo-soprano and piano to texts by the composer, who has written:

The words were selected for their evocative and phonetic properties to conjure up the sense of things experienced: the first, the cry of the loon heard in the North Country, one of the most beautiful and haunting sounds of all Canadian wildlife; second, the brilliance of reflected, shattered light; third, like trying to capture a lopsided rolling ball, the impossibility of capturing spinning time;

14 The choral speaking here on 'Crucify him' is similar to the outbursts of the court-room crowd in act III, scene iv of *Louis Riel*.

6.10 *Evocations*: excerpts from Nos. 1 and 4, showing the use of vowel sounds

fourth, the contracting, cracking, cold winter night as reflection of inner cold; then a *vocalise* in which the pianist strikes the inner ribs of the piano as punctuation and free counterpoint to the voice. A simple phrase: 'In the womb/is contained/the tomb' terminates the piece.[15]

The last song recalls certain words and musical fragments of the first, giving the work a cyclical aspect reminiscent of Twelve Miniatures (for example, the lines 'In the womb/is contained/the tomb' relate to 'Darkness, womb of night.')[16] While the text itself shares certain images with the haiku of the earlier work, the treatment of words, in some cases as pure sound material, is considerably different. This is particularly apparent in the use of vowel sounds in the first and fourth songs (example 6.10). The repeated note figure on 'Loon' in example 6.10a (a marvellously apt idea, as anyone who has heard the bird's cry will know) is actually a free return of the opening section of the song. In between, the piano supplies a delicate tissue of sound, consisting of widely spaced, single notes freely woven around the voice (the text here being 'Mist, wreath of night' and 'infinity of points of light'). Again, silence plays an important role. Many other instances of equally 'evocative' realizations of the text in music could be cited: for instance, the way in which a constant speeding up and slowing down of two rhythmically asymmetrical interval cells in the piano part of the third song suggests a 'lopsided,' elusive quality (see Somers' notes above). Here the technique of

15 From a 'Music of Today' script (n.d.)
16 The entire text of the first song may be found at the beginning of chapter 1.

juxtaposing several small, constant interval cells having a nervous rhythmic irregularity recalls a similar technique in brass and percussion in the middle part of the fifth of the Five Concepts for Orchestra (but without the constant tempo glissandi). Or the bleak, motionless atmosphere created at the beginning of the fourth song by slow clusters in the middle range of the piano, with expressionless, repeated B's in the voice, for the words 'Moon cracks and spreads Winter night,' ending with a slow glissando.

In *Evocations* the range and variety of non-semantic sound material becomes a device to extend the emotions evoked by specific images into a different level of experience. This is particularly true of the latter two-thirds of the fourth song, which is all vowel singing (interrupted by two 'screams or gasps or both' and the spoken phrase 'In the womb/is contained/the tomb'). A section like this clearly foreshadows *Voiceplay*, as does the use of the piano as a resonating echo chamber in the first song. But *Evocations* also reflects the influence of European and American music of the early sixties in a more general sense (Somers had been involved with 'Music of Today' since January 1965). The most obvious manifestation of this, of course, is in the area of rhythm and duration. Throughout the work, durations of sound, silences, and changes of tempi are relative (i.e. not metrically notated) and depend as much on decisions by the performers as on what is notated in the score. Although at the beginning of the third song traditional time values are used (the only section of the work where this is so), the performer is instructed to use them as 'guidelines' only, retaining their 'asymmetrical character.' The fourth song shows further evidence of the encroachment of new attitudes and techniques – while the singer vocalizes on vowel sounds, the pianist is invited to improvise with vibraphone mallets or knuckles on the inner ribs and frame of piano. The word 'invited' is used advisedly here; the score reads 'Pianist could experiment' – a tentative and nonchalant opening move away from strictly notated music.[17] But the appearance of a new kind of aesthetic is also evident in certain sections which consist entirely of a series of discrete musical events, couched in the gestures and sounds of post-Webern serialism. Yet Somers shows even here (as in the second song) no inclination to adhere to a strictly asymmetrical, non-repetitive structure. The basic unit of the extended grace note figure (with tremolo

17 At the end, a bit of graphic notation in the form of a jagged line to suggest the contour and character of the final piano figure, is followed by a written-out version with the caption 'suggestion for tired pianists.'

6.11 *Evocations*: No. 2, basic thematic unit

sometimes added) is a clearly identifiable idea which sticks in the mind and ensures coherence, almost in a thematic sense, despite the discontinuity of the texture (example 6.11).

The possibilities of more extensive improvisation were explored again in 1968 in a work already mentioned in another context – the theatre piece *Improvisation*, commissioned by the CBC for an all-Somers concert in the 1968 CBC Montreal Festival. In the meantime, Somers had included improvised drum interludes in *Louis Riel*, where the score was graphic, indicating the general shape of musical events by the density of a succession of diminishing dots. In *Improvisation*, graphic notation is used in two of the seven sections, to suggest in a general way the nature of particular events and textures (for instance, 'tutti chords' are indicated by single vertical lines which are grouped so as to indicate density of texture; the content of vertical aggregates will be indeterminate). But the rest of the score is really a 'map,' presenting the performers with a framework of actions and sound materials by way of verbal descriptions for each stage of the proceedings. In the prefatory notes, Somers states: 'The improvisation should provide both audience and performers with a measure of pleasure, fun and excitement in reacting to the unpremeditated and unforeseen. For the musician it will be an experiment, a test of musical reflexes and, I hope, discovery.' The performers consist of four singers (SATB), strings and woodwinds (the exact number of which is not specified), two percussionists, pianist (using two pianos, one prepared, the other unprepared), narrator (Somers himself in the two performances to date), and conductor.

Improvisation consists of 'dissociation,' in which several strands or layers of interrelated musical events and physical gestures proceed simultaneously among the various performers and groups, intersecting at certain points, and 'interaction,' in which performers react and respond to each other, triggering new situations which carry the events into new directions.

In a sense, the gestures of traditional music and its performance

situation are disassembled and rearranged, with unexpected and sometimes humorous results. For example, the equivalent in *Improvisation*
of an instrumental solo after a tutti crescendo and climax in a traditional piece is provided by the pianist dropping ping pong balls on to the
piano strings, with sostenuto pedal down (after a kind of tutti build-up
of activity). Or the traditional manner of orchestral performers walking
on stage before a performance and warming up becomes the basis of an
extended sequence in itself at the opening of *Improvisation*. Gradually
performers approach the stage from the foyer, from among the audience,
and from the wings of the stage. While the strings silently mime as
though playing (actually thinking of a particular piece), the narrator
wanders on stage, talking about various aspects of the work (as mentioned earlier, Somers used a tennis ball for this as a kind of stage prop),
and is gradually drowned out by singers and woodwinds. At the end, all
performers exit at random, whispering, and leaving a sole string player
on stage miming performance (as at the beginning). Here again, one
notes a tendency to 'cyclical' structure (in contrast to the 'open-ended'
structure of much recent music).

The singers in this work (and sometimes the instrumentalists) use
as text and sound material excerpts from Shakespeare's *Tempest* and
Yeats' *Needle's Eye*. This material is used in a number of ways – shouting or singing random words; extending the sound potential of words
(sibilants, vowels, consonants) into values; or presenting a direct version of a text on one level (spoken or sung) against another level
involving one of the previous methods or different sound material altogether. Thus, the texts add yet another dimension or layer of possibilities to levels involving only physical gestures and instrumental
sounds, making the texture all the richer and more capable of building
tension or creating unexpected twists and turns.

Obviously, one's reaction to a work such as *Improvisation* is deter-
mined by personal tastes and aesthetic concepts. Traditionalists found
the work 'insubstantial,' a predictable reaction, since it lacked any
obvious characteristics of nineteenth-century European music. Others,
such as Gilles Potvin, found the work sophisticated and stimulating, and
a testament to 'the vitality of musical creativity in Canada.'[18] For
Somers, *Improvisation* represented a major (and in the opinion of this
writer, successful) step into the areas of indeterminacy and music
theatre, both of which had been extensively explored in the United

18 Gilles Potvin *La Presse*, Montreal, 8 July 1968

States and Europe during the fifties and early sixties. Typically, his exploration of this aesthetic, so far removed from that of his earlier music, came about through a long process of re-evaluation and evolution, rather than a desire to adopt an *avant-garde* stance.

Since *Improvisation*, the only work that extensively uses improvisation and chance procedures has been *And*, commissioned by CBC television for the Toronto Dance Theatre. Here, a small ensemble, consisting of vocal quartet (SATB), flute, harp, piano, and four percussionists, improvise upon what Somers refers to as 'mosaics' – small units of written musical ideas, drawings, and suggestions. The choreographic outline (suggesting the life cycle of man, from birth to death, in an ancient pagan civilization) was loose enough to permit interaction between the musicians and dancers.

7
Louis Riel

There is little doubt that Somers' most important achievement to date is the three act opera *Louis Riel*, not only because the work was a spectacular success with both audiences and critics (including a rave review in the influential journal *Opernwelt*), but because it is a synthesis of virtually every important aspect of Somers' writing since *North Country*. As early as 1963 the possibility of an opera based on the controversial Métis leader occurred to the publishing executive and arts patron, Floyd Chalmers, and the actor, playwright, and director, Mavor Moore. By 1965 an opera based on Louis Riel with libretto by Mavor Moore and music by Harry Somers had been commissioned for the Canadian Opera Company by the Floyd S. Chalmers Foundation. Additional financial backing was provided by the Centennial Commission, the Canada Council, and the Ontario Arts Council. The work was to be ready for performance in 1967, Canada's centennial year.[1]

The choice of Louis Riel as the subject of an opera to be performed during Canada's centennial celebrations was appropriate. For many years Riel has been considered a potent symbol of various divisive forces which have shaped Canada. These not only include the 'love-hate' relationship between French- and English-speaking peoples but, as R. Murray Schafer points out in his study of *Riel*'s public impact through the media, the tensions between 'native and white, church and state,

1 Another opera, *The Firebrand*, based on the Toronto political reformer William Lyon Mackenzie (1795–1861), was commissioned by the CBC, but never got past the planning stages. Somers felt that the libretto was not suitable for operatic treatment.

colonialism and independence, civilization and frontier wilderness.'[2] If Riel personifies 'the dissonance at the root of the Canadian temperament' (to use Schafer's phrase), he also represents certain aspects of the human condition which are timeless and universal. Mavor Moore has described Riel as an 'immensely colourful personification of some of the great liturgical themes of mankind ... the idealist driven mad ... the thinker paralyzed by his thinking, the Hamlet syndrome ... the half-breed, the schizophrenic outsider ... the leader of a small nation standing in the way of progress.'[3]

The work received its *première* on 23 September 1967 at Toronto's O'Keefe Centre, and seven more live performances followed (including two in Montreal as part of Expo 67's 'World Festival') – a record for any Canadian grand opera.[4] For this production, the best stage and musical talents in Canada were assembled. Stage direction was by Leon Major, with sets designed by Murray Laufer and costumes by Marie Day. One of the most memorable aspects of the production was the imaginative staging: fragmented, three-dimensional sets, photo blow-ups, painted backgrounds, and slide projections were designed to produce a stylized, super-realistic effect. Somers' longtime friend and an enthusiastic champion of new Canadian music, Victor Feldbrill, conducted. The cast included Bernard Turgeon as Riel, Joseph Rouleau as Bishop Taché, Cornelis Opthof as Sir John A. Macdonald, Patricia Rideout as Riel's mother Julie, Mary Morrison as his sister Sara, and Roxolana Roslak as his wife Marguerite (a role for which she received special praise).

Two years later, on 29 October 1969, the entire opera was telecast in colour over the full CBC-TV English network. This version, produced by Franz Kraemer, retained for the most part the same cast and stage personnel, but made certain adjustments in staging and costumes to accommodate the television medium.[5] Some reviewers (in the Toronto area) felt that many of the flaws of the earlier stage version had been overcome in the move from stage to film. One critic wrote that the shifts between the two centres of action, Ottawa and the West, could be negotiated more smoothly on television, resulting in a 'more fluid continuity.'[6] Another believed that television was 'the ideal fate' of the

2 *Louis Riel* 18   3 CBC *Times* 25–31 October 1969, 4–5
4 The breakdown of performances: three in Toronto (September-October 1967), two in Montreal (October 1967), three in Toronto (September-October 1968). Total attendance for the eight performances was 19,933.
5 For a summary of these, see Graham 'Louis Riel' 4–5.
6 *Toronto Daily Star* 28 October 1969

work, with its 'scenario-type libretto ... and super film-score music,' and that certain unoperatic scenes gained in effectiveness and vividness on television. Critics in Western Canada were somewhat less than sympathetic to the entire undertaking. About thirteen per cent of the entire viewing audience for the evening of the telecast watched the opera. Of those, a large majority were totally negative about the production.[7]

At the core of the opera are the circumstances surrounding two related events: the execution in 1869 of Thomas Scott, a fanatic Orangeman, at the hands of Riel and his Métis followers, and the execution of Riel himself in 1885 by the Canadian authorities. The reasons used by Riel to justify Scott's execution, and by Sir John A. Macdonald, the prime minister, to justify that of Riel, form a motif which lends a sense of dramatic irony to the whole opera. Riel says that he 'cannot let one man stand against a nation'; fifteen years later, Sir John refuses to grant the condemned Riel a reprieve for the same reason – 'I cannot let one foolish man stand in the way of a whole nation.' This irony is also reflected in the circumstances surrounding the trial of each man: in both cases, the odds were heavily stacked against the defendants by legal improprieties and racial prejudice. However, Moore also saw in the wit and pragmatism of Macdonald, the political realist, an opportunity to provide a satirical element to balance the heavy drama of the central figure and the events which befall him. Thus, Sir John emerges at times as a slightly silly political opportunist given to immoderate imbibing and bad punning ('Touché, Taché' – an example quoted in many history books). Since the events of the opera involve French- and English-speaking characters, Moore decided to write a libretto in both French and English (and to a lesser extent, Cree and Latin), using whichever language was appropriate to the character at a given moment. For the French parts of the libretto, Moore collaborated with the Montreal playwright Jacques Languirand.[8]

A detailed account of the musical and dramatic structure of this complex work would in itself require a complete book. A brief scene-by-scene synopsis of the plot, together with the important musical characteristics of each scene is given in appendix 3 (pp. 167–72). For Somers, the problems posed by the multiplicity of contrasts, tensions, and themes within the libretto translated themselves into a score in which

7 For further information about public reaction, see Schafer *Louis Riel* 25–7
8 For more on various conceptual ideas and problems in the work, see the condensed transcript of a conversation between Somers, Mavor Moore, Herman Geiger-Torel, and Keith MacMillan in *Musicanada* 4 (September 1967): 5–6, 12.

7.1 *Louis Riel*: a/ act II, scene vi; b/ act I, scene iii, four bars after |8|

diversity became the most important factor. This meant not only a diversity of style (i.e. the juxtaposition and superimposition of different musical styles, as in the fifties), but the use of different types of voice production and presentation (ranging from speech to full singing) as a means of identifying character. This technique is somewhat analogous to that used in *The Fool* (combined there within one character). In *Riel*, different types of voice delivery are used to highlight the juxtaposition of Riel and Macdonald: Riel, the visionary and romanticist, sings; Macdonald, the 'political realist, the pragmatist,' as Somers called him, sings at times, but for the most part expresses himself in a more prosaic kind of 'sung speech' – 'a rather satirical form of speech ... heightened, inflected, and ... guided.'[9] For conversational purposes, in both types of delivery (and this applies to other characters as well), Somers evolved a highly flexible, *parlando* kind of presentation which at times lies very close to recitative, following the natural inflections and rhythms of speech. Example 7.1 provides brief illustrations of this as seen in Riel and Macdonald. The excerpt quoted in example 7.1a represents a middle-of-the-road kind of delivery for Riel – his part fluctuates widely between recitative on one or two repeated notes and the highly melismatic, lyrical singing in his solo arias (for example act I, scene iv). Other

9 Ibid 6

characters as well show considerable differences in manner of singing. Among the three women in Riel's life, Marguerite, his Cree wife, alternates between a melismatic, lyrical style, with fairly wide range, featuring ornamental decorations and inflections and syllabic, rhythmically accented reiterations of a single pitch (in 'Kuyas,' act III, scene i), while Julie and Sara Riel approximate the style of Riel as shown above – a kind of arioso.

Somers has described *Louis Riel* as a multi-level work. This can be seen in two ways. First of all, the orchestral accompaniment to a particular scene may not 'accompany' in the sense of imitating or reinforcing the voice. It may instead present a different layer of meaning, as in some of the political scenes in Ottawa, in which the dialogue is accompanied by banal dance music. The second and most important kind of multi-layered writing involves the use of a number of different stylistic approaches juxtaposed and/or superimposed, each having a special significance in a given situation – one to impart an authentic, realistic flavour (as in native peoples' scenes), another to underline a certain aspect of a dramatic situation by the use of a style familiar to the audience (as in the crowd-haranguing scene at the railway depot in act II, scene iii), or by contrast, yet another to jar the audience with an unfamiliar style, again to heighten the dramatic impact.

Four stylistic approaches are used in the work (the terms of classification are Somers' own): abstract, atonal orchestral writing; electronically produced sounds; folk material; and straight diatonic writing.

Abstract, atonal orchestral writing is used 'for dramatic intensity and to create a platform of orchestral sound on top of which the singing is entirely apart.'[10] This, of course, is Somers' own style as evidenced in orchestral works of the early sixties – strongly dissonant, with two basic types of material: nervous rhythmic figures (often entrusted to brass) and sustained single pitches or vertical aggregates with pronounced individual dynamic fluctuations. This type of writing occurs in scenes set in the West; for example, the introduction and scene i of act I, or the two scenes in act II concerning the trial and execution of Thomas Scott.

The electronically produced sounds were created in collaboration with Lowell Cross in the Electronic Music Studio at the University of Toronto. Somers himself has stated that it was his original intention to use this material in four places to achieve 'a certain kind of impact by

10 *CBC Times* 25–31 October 1969, 4–5

Molto Lento

7.2 *Louis Riel*: opening section of 'Kuyas' from act III, scene i

presenting the audience with a totally unfamiliar sound.' This was to occur during the opera's introduction (to prepare for the tension of the first scene), during a battle interlude in act III, between scenes iii and iv, and during Riel's two most extensive and intensive arias: in the last scene of act I, where Riel sees himself as the prophet David, and in the trial scene in act III. Here, Somers has written that he

> wanted to achieve something Kafka-ish rather than literal: the prosecuted man who really doesn't understand the frame of reference he's in. The voices from the speakers, sometimes totally distorted, sound various statements and accusations while Riel keeps trying to sing over and through them.[11]

In the end, however, he retained electronic material only for the battle scene and introduction, preferring instead to allow Riel's voice and the listener's imagination to create the desired effect.

There are two categories of folk material – native peoples' music and popular songs from white society of the period. The most important example of native peoples' music is Marguerite's aria 'Kuyas' (Cree Indian for 'long ago'). The motivic basis for this song, presented in the opening five or six notes, was taken from the song of Skateen, the Wolfhead chief of a Nass River Tribe, as collected and notated by Marius Barbeau and Sir Ernest MacMillan.[12] Somers regards it as a lament for the passing of a people. As can be seen from the opening section (example 7.2), the style of vocal writing (in this and certain other sections) is similar to that of *Evocations* – melismas on vowels and extensive use of small ornaments. Intervallic movement, around a framework of E–B, is by seconds and thirds. Later, a sparse rhythmic accompaniment is pro-

11 Ibid 4
12 Published in V.E. Garfield *The Tsimshian: Their Arts and Music* New York, J.J. Augustin 1951. *Kuyas* has been published separately (Berandol 1971).

7.3 *Louis Riel*: first two phrases of the introduction to act I

vided by flute, sleigh bells, medium pitch tom-tom, and tenor and bass drums. In other parts of the opera, the distinctive timbres of these instruments are associated with specific moods and scenes, and thus play a quasi-motivic role throughout. The other native people's music in the opera occurs at the beginning of the final scene of act II, in the form of two Indian dances. The words and music of the second of these (called 'The Buffalo Hunt') were drawn from the collection by Margaret Arnett MacLeod in *Songs of Old Manitoba*.[13]

Several popular songs of the Riel period provide material for larger groups of people (for example, a group of Métis or a band of soldiers) and are often superimposed on another style of music (usually the 'atonal' kind). Some of these songs recur throughout the opera, providing further coherence as well as period colour: 'Est-il rien sur la terre?' (in act I, scene ii and act II, scene ii); 'Le Roi malheureux' (act II, scene ii), taken from *Songs of Old Manitoba*; and 'We'll Hang Him up the River,' which occurs first in the crowd-haranguing scene (act II, scene iv) and recurs at the end of act II and after Riel's trial scene. This song was used, with permission, from John Coulter's play *Riel* (the music was notated by Dr Healey Willan from a version Coulter recalled from his youth in Ireland). At its final appearance, after Riel's trial scene, it takes on a considerably more vicious, chilling character, to indicate the crowd's thirst for blood (also made apparent by the trial crowd's hysterical outbursts, which form a kind of ostinato layer throughout act III, scene iv). A more subtle transformation of material over the entire opera can be seen in the treatment of the song (prerecorded by Somers himself) at the beginning of the opera (example 7.3). Somers has described this song, sung by soldiers who were heading out west in 1869, as a 'core moving out through the whole work.' It first reappears as an intense melodic line in the violins, in four phrases separated by brief improvised

13 Toronto, Ryerson Press 1960

7.4 *Louis Riel*: act i, scene i, interlude

7.5 *Louis Riel*: act i, scene ii

outbursts from tom-toms, as at the very beginning of the opera (example 7.4). The line's dynamic 'restlessness' and climax-oriented contour (rising by small intervals and rounded off by a falling semitone) show how thoroughly Somers transformed borrowed material and made it his own. The minor third at the beginning subsequently reappears as the basis of a recurring flute solo (example 7.5) which surfaces from time to time, generally at points of transition, as a kind of lonely comment (reminder?) before or after a point of high tension. The return, at the very end of the opera, of a simplified version of the opening phrase (again as a flute solo) is especially poignant.

Straight diatonic writing occurs chiefly in two places: at the opening of act iii, scene ii, in which Father André and his parishioners are celebrating Maundy Thursday Mass, and during the crowd-haranguing scene in act ii, scene iv. The latter scene, at the railway depot in Toronto, contains some of the few comic touches in the entire opera (outside of those involving Sir John A.). Dr Schultz and Charles Mair, the leaders of the Canadian Party in Red River, come to Ontario to whip up sympathy for their cause by making the recently executed Scott look like a martyr for Canada. Somers felt that in order to give the scene an underlying quality of cynicism and wit, he had to use a style of music that the audience could recognize – i.e. diatonic music with a tune. Thus, at the beginning of the scene, the crowd sings a rousing chorus beginning with the words 'Canada first; Canada is British. Oh Or'ngemen unite.' The music itself is of the hymn-tune type – or 'central Ontario Gothic' (to use Somers' term). An on-stage band (clarinet, cornet, tuba, and drum) accompanies this, playing very badly. When Schultz begins to harangue the crowd, the band stikes up again with a very saccharine Victorian tune (played on the cornet). For Somers this implied sinister overtones lurking beneath the surface drollery – the use of banal associations to arouse mass patriotism.

As already indicated, the different styles of music described above do not form separate entities, one following upon the other, but rather flow in and out of each other, with considerable dovetailing and superimposition of layers, in addition to straight juxtaposition. For example, after Marguerite's aria 'Kuyas,' when messengers arrive from Saskatchewan, the orchestra returns abruptly to the 'abstract, atonal' style and thereby immediately evokes associations with earlier events in Riel's life. Yet the materials – rhythms, melodic shapes, and motives (including the ornaments) – of 'Kuyas' persist until the end of the scene, thus vividly projecting the struggle for Riel's commitment. The opera, then, is not simply a pastiche of various musical styles, not only for the reason outlined above, but because the essence of the music which recurs again and again and impresses itself most powerfully on the listener's consciousness is Somers' own style, i.e. the so-called abstract, atonal writing.

Many instances could be cited of the dramatic power and richness of these parts of the score (which one critic ungraciously referred to as 'ugly stereophonic noises'). In the introduction to the opera, for instance, two layers of sound are superimposed, one orchestral, the other electronic; these weave in and out of each other and set up the tension-filled atmosphere of the first scene. The orchestral layer is a direct descendant of the orchestral works of the early sixties – the very opening, for instance, with its sustained clusters in the strings 'attacked' by isolated splinter-like sonorities in brass and woodwinds, could easily fit into the opening string orchestra section of *Stereophony*. This breaks off abruptly to make way for a new build-up composed of layers of single sustained pitches, each of which has an individual duration and dynamic envelope (rather like Nono's *Il canto sospeso*). In the final section, solid blocks of sonority move from one orchestral group to another, in fact forming a live counterpoint to what the electronic sounds are doing; the close identity of sound material here vividly points up the influence of electronic music on Somers' orchestral writing of the early sixties. The way in which this material leads into the first scene, by way of isolated percussion fragments (along with remnants of the earlier sustained material) is striking: gradually the sustained elements in the strings move into a high chromatic tetrachord in the violins, which provide an eerie background for sporadic, delicate interpolations

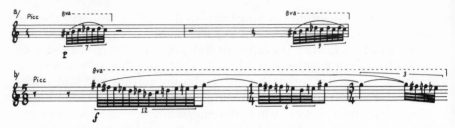

7.6 *Louis Riel*: a/ act I, scene i; b/ act III, scene iii

by harp, piccolo, timpani, tam-tam, bongo, cymbals, and sleigh-bells. This produces a spooky, suspense-laden atmosphere for the confrontation between the rebels and McDougall (whose rather sweeping, rhetorical manner of singing contrasts sharply with the orchestral accompaniment).

Exactly the same material is repeated in act III, scene iii, another 'confrontation,' this time between Riel and Father André. At first the orchestral texture is thin as before. Once Riel begins his monologue (recounting a dream and praying for divine help to defeat the forces of Satan), the texture gradually thickens into a whirling, rushing mass of sound, suggesting the madness underlying his action and words. The basis for the material in this section is the tiny piccolo fragment of act I, scene i, now expanded into a continuous arabesque which extends throughout the orchestra (example 7.6). The orchestral-electronic introduction to the first act appears again (intact) between scenes iii and iv of act III as an interlude suggesting the battle between rebels and government forces (in the production this was suggested through slides and photographs).[14]

The music of the Ottawa scenes (featuring the political machinations of Sir John A.) is, by contrast, lighter in mood as well as in actual orchestral weight. Somers envisaged these scenes as a kind of vaudeville or political dance. The rhythms here not only are dance-like and banal ('like a fairly slow dance tempo') but have a vague lilt which gives the music a quality Somers later dubbed 'Sir-John-slightly-high.' The music itself does not adhere to a tonal centre or framework, but achieves its charm and wit by discreet tonal references. The clearest precedent for

14 A similar comparison could be made of the two trial scenes. In both the music powerfully underlines the essential dramatic structure. In Scott's trial, for instance, a Kafka-like atmosphere was achieved by limiting material to low harp, tam-tam, and tom-tom sounds which gradually accumulate tension, then break off to single wood-block 'ticks' to mark the heavy passing of time before the sentencing.

7.7 *Louis Riel*: act I, scene iii

7.8 *Louis Riel*: act I, scene iii, four bars after 8

this kind of writing in Somers' own music is in the second subject of the Symphony No. 1. (Compare, for instance the 'theme' in example 7.7 to theme s2d in the symphony.) All of these qualities can be seen in one of Sir John's most important and characteristic themes which accompanies his first appearance in the opera in act I, scene iii (example 7.7). One of the many transformations this theme undergoes is shown in example 7.8. Later in the scene, composer and librettist give full rein to the vaudeville analogy by having Sir John indulge in a kind of distorted vaudeville song, beginning with the lines:

Sugar is the oil for political machines:
Without it all the gears would never mesh
A man must have a weakness
For a certain kind of sweetness
Be it soothing to the spirit or the flesh.

Act II begins with more 'Sir-John-slightly-high' music, composed of various themes from the earlier scene and woven into a thick maze of motives and countermotives which ultimately collapse into a tuba solo. Sir John's music does not, however, remain at the same flippant level throughout the opera. In act II, scene v, a new thematic idea is added (example 7.9) with Macdonald's words 'The Colonel's job is to protect all citizens of whatever hue.' This theme becomes one of the dominant

7.9 *Louis Riel*: act II, scene v

strands of the very last scene of the opera, in which Taché and Lemieux are pleading with Sir John for a reprieve for Riel. This time, the theme is part of a multi-layered texture (including an eleventh chord brass figure which previously announced Ottawa scenes) and takes on a sinister and tragic character, as the final movements of the opera build into a huge climax ending with the announcement of Riel's death. These relationships between text, music, and dramatic structure thus show a further sense of irony underlying the whole opera (i.e. the protection of 'all citizens of whatever hue' evidently does not extend as far as granting fair trials to all).

Somers deliberately called *Louis Riel* a music drama, intending that the music be a 'kind of stream to keep the dramatic flow going during sequences of events and actions.' When these reached points of repose, the music would have a chance to 'sing out'; these points are marked by the dances at the beginning of act III, scene vi, and more importantly by the solo arias of Louis and Marguerite. The peaks of dramatic tension throughout the score – such as Scott's trial and the scene following in which Sara and Julie attempt to make Riel call off the execution – form a counterpoint to the solo arias (really soliloquies) which have a different kind of tension of their own, based primarily on the musical structure of a single line. This, in turn, reflects the tension implied by the text, often illuminating a certain state of mind. The most powerful of these is Riel's soliloquy at the end of the first act, a kind of 'nightmarish' (Mavor Moore's term) version of one of the psalms from the Bible. The style of singing here is impassioned throughout, even frenzied towards the end, alternating between recitative and very florid melismas, trailing off between phrases and at the end into slides or sung speech. This projection of Riel's vision into a single, tension-packed line, supported sparsely by single sustained violin pitches (with the crescendo dynamic envelope), is one of the most striking, intense moments in the opera.

It is good to know that *Louis Riel* will not suffer the neglect accorded to so much twentieth-century music. It was revived for the 1975 season of the Canadian Opera Company.

8

Rome 1969-71 and the early seventies

At the end of the sixties, Somers was deeply involved in a number of projects. In addition to being special consultant to the North York Board of Education during the 1968–9 school year (see chapter 6), he was involved with several new works in various stages of completion: a *Missa brevis* for the CBC's Department of Religious Broadcasts (much later to become the *Kyrie*); *And*, a ballet commissioned by CBC television for the Toronto Dance Theatre; and a work for Cathy Berberian, also commissioned by the CBC. In addition he was contemplating a fourth string quartet (which has not, however, materialized). In June of 1969 *Louis Riel* was scheduled to be taped for CBC television. In September of 1967 (the day after the first performance of *Louis Riel*) he married the distinguished Canadian actress and co-founder of Toronto's Crest Theatre, Barbara Chilcott. Miss Chilcott's diverse interests have added new dimensions to his own work. *Voiceplay*, for instance, was a direct outgrowth of their discussions about the possibilities of musically adapting the way an actor uses his voice for the stage. And her interest in Eastern religion and philosophy (she had been a student of the Maharishi Mahesh Yogi at Rishikish, Kashmir, as early as 1960) renewed his contact with an area of thought with which he had not been actively concerned since his youth.

In April 1969, the Canadian Cultural Institute in Rome, acting on the advice of the Canada Council, awarded two $18,000 grants, one to Somers and the other to the Montreal designer Julien Hébert.[1] The

---

1 The award came about through a 1966 arrangement whereby the Italian government placed $500,000 at the Canadian government's disposal, with the idea that the income from the fund would be used to foster cultural ties between the two countries.

award stipulated only that the recipients spend their time (and the money) in Italy. For Somers, the honour was a timely opportunity to escape from the hectic pace of Toronto and immerse himself in a totally foreign environment, one in which he could simply 'contemplate his creative navel.' It was not until October 1969 that Somers and his wife were able to fulfil their commitments in Toronto and leave for Rome.

They rented a spacious apartment which turned out to be next door to an ancient house-turned-convent. At 6:15 AM each day the bells would begin ringing, to the accompaniment of the nuns and a few priests chanting their morning prayers: 'The voices are not raised to God in the refined and sophisticated manner of Solomon, but their song is somehow compensated for by a solid earth-rooted devotion devoid of such nonsense as perfect intonation.'[2] The bell sounds were an important component of that city's total sound environment and eventually filtered through into Somers' own creative work; in Kyrie he makes extensive use of gongs and reverberating instruments. The impact made on him by this new world of sound is vividly described in the letter to the Canada Music Book, quoted from above. This letter corroborates Victor Feldbrill's observation (to this writer) that for Somers life is 'a constant construction of sound,' to be experienced in totality as a rich source of creative nourishment.

The nuns next door provided some lighter moments, as well as an intriguing glimpse into the subtleties of the Italian language, as the following portion of a letter to Eric Aldwinckle shows:

Your [Aldwinckle's] lady who empties slops over the 10th storey balcony is also here in the land of Leonardo, in spite of his inventions. It happened from an upper story of this building onto an ancient, but broad beamed nun next door shortly she had emerged from chanting early morning prayers to her God in some Baroque heaven. She reacted in a very worldly fashion and I received a thorough education in the richness of Italian.[3]

He began studying Italian as soon as he arrived, and soon became proficient enough to begin reading Dante's Divina Commedia, a work which deeply impressed him with the 'beauty and depth of its imagery and symbolism.'[4] In addition, he was reading Susanne Langer's Feeling and Form, which he believes has clarified his own thinking considerably

2 'A Letter from Rome' 105   3 16 January 1970
4 Letter to Eric Aldwinckle, 17 May 1970. A portion of the same letter is quoted at the beginning of chapter 1.

during the past few years. But an equally potent catalyst to his own writing was his rediscovery of Bach's *Well-Tempered Clavier*: 'Practising the wt sets my own mind in order to do my own work ... no matter what tempo one takes them at, they always make sense and always reveal some startling stroke of genius. Bach must have known creative fulfilment as few in this world have ever known (and I'm not just talking about us little kids).'[5]

During the two years he spent in Rome, he was introduced to some Italian composers by an exceptional Japanese-born singer and performer of contemporary music, Michiko Hirayama, whom he met at the American Institute. Through Somers, Miss Hirayama became interested in contemporary Canadian music, and in the fall of 1970 she visited Toronto in order to become better acquainted with Canadian music and some of its leading personalities. The ultimate outcome of this contact was a concert of Canadian music in Rome in May of 1972, including works by Somers, Norma Beecroft, John Hawkins, R. Murray Schafer, and John Weinzweig. In the fall of 1971, Somers and his wife returned to Canada by way of a three-month visit to India, Nepal, Thailand, and Bali, which was undertaken in order for him to experience oriental music first-hand. This exposure has already played an important role in two new works: *Chura-churum*, in progress during 1972–3, for the Swingle Singers and the Montreal Symphony Orchestra, and *Music for Solo Violin*, a work commissioned by Yehudi Menuhin for the 1974 Guelph Spring Festival.

Two new works resulted from the Rome experience – *Voiceplay* and the *Kyrie*. Both were the result, in part, of his experiences during the late sixties – the work in the schools, the use of new vocal techniques, and the gathering of elements of theatre and improvisation into his writing. But these experiences were filtered through a long process of thought and maturation made possible by the Rome 'sabbatical.'

Voiceplay, completed in 1971, was commissioned by the cbc for Cathy Berberian and first performed by her in 1972 in Toronto. The origins of the work can be traced back to a lecture Somers had been asked to deliver at a symposium of student composers held at McGill University in 1969. The lecture was one of three dealing with various aspects of contemporary vocal writing. Instead of presenting a straight lecture, Somers decided to demonstrate the wide range of vocal possibilities in

8.1 *Voiceplay* (in the composer's hand)

the form of a progression of sounds from 'breath' noises to fully sung, and back to breath sounds again. As no one had been warned, and he was the last to speak, the impact of his 'lecture' was considerable. At the end, he responded to questions from the floor with more non-verbal and sung sounds. In *Voiceplay* certain theatrical elements were added to the basic skeleton of this lecture, in order to provide dramatic shape and coherence to what might otherwise have been a mere catalogue of voice techniques, as well as to establish communication between audience and performer.

The lecture format not only provides a framework within which *Voiceplay* begins and ends, but helps to determine certain modes of behaviour and presentation for both soloist and accompanist throughout the work. Thus, the accompanist (who need not be a regular singer's accompanist) introduces the performer at the beginning, as one would an ordinary lecturer, and thanks him or her at the end, rounding off the presentation by asking for questions from the audience (as had occurred at McGill). During the 'performance,' the accompanist acts as assistant, for instance helping with and describing a series of limbering-up exercises. The main burden of the work, however, falls to the soloist.

The soloist is required to play four different roles, the identities of which may overlap, combine, or remain separate: lecturer, demonstrator, actor or actress, and singer. In addition, the soloist must sometimes present symbols of what Somers has called 'objective and subjective states.'[6] In the objective state, the soloist demonstrates vocal resources and physical exercises, and relates facts. There is no emotional involvement here – everything is externalized, while the audience

6 From Somers' own notes to the score, on which this paragraph is based

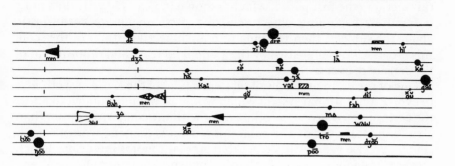

merely observes. This occurs, for example, during the second of the work's sixteen sections, in which the soloist matter-of-factly begins to demonstrate 'head' sounds (here 'colour-tone hums'). In areas involving 'subjective' states, the soloist is emotionally involved, presenting internal states of fear, panic, anxiety, 'with which the audience may identify and to which it reacts.' In the seventh section, for instance, the soloist, playing actor, projects a three-way conversation, using sibilants, unvoiced phonetic vowel sounds, and tiny hummed fragments. These two 'states' may be combined, or flow almost imperceptibly from one into the other, as for example, when the soloist performs various 'limbering-up' exercises, which not only free various resonating cavities in a physical sense, but suggest in the soloist – now actor – a flow of emotion culminating in hysteria.

The sound material for *Voiceplay* is extremely varied. Some indication of the enormous range of possibilities (and the extremes of unvoiced and voiced sounds) is presented at the beginning, when the soloist 'tests' the microphone with two gently unvoiced exhalations, then follows with a sudden judo exclamation ('guaranteed to wake up an audience,' as Somers remarks in his notes). The main nucleus of sound material consists of phonetic sounds: thirteen vowels, presented unvoiced (whispered) and voiced, and twenty-six consonants. These are not only used by themselves as raw material, separately and combined, but in conjunction with 'breath' sounds, sibilants ('s' and 'sh'), hummed colour tones, and towards the end, with fully voiced singing. The thirteen vowels, if whispered in a certain order, produce a scale of thirteen successive pitches from low to high which become specific compositional factors. This may be seen, for example, in the fourth section, in which unvoiced consonant-vowel combinations (producing a set of rising pitch relationships) alternate with colour-tone hums. In this section (the first part of which is shown in example 8.1), the soloist is lecturer, beginning objectively and becoming more enthusiastic about the subject, then relaxing into an 'objective' state. In the score this progression is indicated by the gradual increase and thinning out of the density of events.

One of the main problems of this work (and of the *Kyrie* as well) was to evolve a notational system which would be flexible enough to allow the performer to become a collaborator with the composer (rather than a subordinate), yet at the same time use (in Somers' words) 'clear, simple, precise geometric shapes to represent sonoral intentions which are not ambiguous, can be almost immediately comprehended, and which clearly fix in the mind a visual image of the sonoral intention: shapes which can be responded to on an immediate and intuitive basis.' These notational symbols evolved, at least in part, from his work in the schools in 1968–9. Thus, voiced colour tones (hummed or sung) are indicated in the following manner:

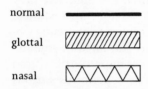

A gradual transition from one to the other is indicated thus:

When appropriate, obvious diagrammatic notation is used, as in the 'limbering-up' exercises in sections 10, 11, and 12, or to indicate various widths and speeds of the opening and closing of the lips:

Both pitch and duration are relative, and temporal proportions play an important role in making the performer's contribution to the work creative and flexible, since the speed with which a page is scanned will vary according to performer, mood, and other considerations.

Voiceplay will mean something different to each person who experiences it, depending on a myriad of subtle factors ranging from psychological and emotional make-up to musical/theatrical background and aesthetic outlook. The work defies any single explanation. Somers believes, in fact, that it should *not* be explained to the audience, that they should approach it on their own terms.

The piece is a display of the vocal range and possibilities of each particular soloist. The piece is a musical 'composition.'
    The piece is a work for theatre.
    The piece will sometimes seem clear in intent to the audience, sometimes an enigma, sometimes ambiguous, sometimes seeming to move in and out of 'focus.'[7]

As mentioned above, *Voiceplay* is an outgrowth and continuation of certain areas of exploration of the late sixties, the most obvious antecedent being *Improvisation*. Besides the theatrical and sound material connections (which are of course far more tightly controlled in *Voiceplay*), both works seem to move (towards the end) from the non-semantic use of language, to isolated coherent statements (for example, in *Voiceplay*, the formal announcement: 'Ancient and modern necromancy alias mesmerism and hypnotism denounced'). However, there are indications as well, of links with other more general aspects of Somers' earlier music. In *Voiceplay*, the constant flow back and forth between 'subjective' and 'objective' states, and the tension which results from this, recall the balancing of emotional drive and intellectual control which is characteristic of so much of his music during the fifties and sixties and which becomes a tension-producing factor. Consider, for example, the abrupt switch in scene ii of *The Fool* from the motet 'Where is my judgement and my strength?' (an objectification of intense feeling) to the 'confrontation' between the King and the Fool immediately afterwards. A parallel opposition occurs, in reversed order, at one of the main climaxes of *Voiceplay*, when the soloist's limbering-up exercises release an emotional flow which evolves into hysterial laughter, to be followed by a return to the 'objective' lecturer's role. In both these cases the audience's responses and expectations are being manipulated, although of course the style juxtaposition factor is missing in *Voiceplay*. It is also worth noting that in *Voiceplay*, as in more traditionally oriented early works, there is a definite sense of building towards a peak – not only in the above-mentioned outburst of hysterical laughter, but in the emergence, during the latter part of the

7 From Somers' notes to *Voiceplay*

work, of the 'singer' role, resulting in ecstatic, fully sung cascades of sound. And finally, the incorporation of theatrical elements was a logical development for a composer who has demonstrated again and again the ability to project an element of drama into even purely instrumental works as far back as the Symphony No. 1 and the Passacaglia and Fugue. In this respect, it is important to emphasize that *Voiceplay* is a work to be seen as well as heard, in order to lend full impact to the four roles which the soloist portrays.

Voiceplay has been followed by two large-scale vocal works. The first of these, the *Kyrie*, was originally intended to be a ten-minute *Missa brevis*, commissioned by CBC television for religious programming, but instead turned out to be a complex twenty-five-minute work. It was begun in Rome early in 1970 and completed about two years later. The scoring involves soprano, alto, tenor, and baritone soloists, full chorus, and an instrumental group comprising solo flute, oboe, clarinet and cello, three trumpets, piano, and six percussionists. Somers has provided the following synopsis of the work:

The basic phrases, 'Kyrie eleison, Christe eleison,' are presented in very many permutations and combinations of their letters and phonetic structure. This stems from a conviction that the meaning of words of ancient origin is in their sound, and not necessarily in the order that has been handed down to us. That somewhere in the permutations and combinations of the neumes which comprise the sounds of the phrases is hidden the inner meaning, which can only be experienced, not 'explained' in the 'semantical' sense.

The vocal techniques employed have evolved over the previous years in my writing. In sections a high degree of complexity is involved both in duration and pitch. As many as fifteen different tempi, all specifically gauged, are combined simultaneously, and working in tonal fabrics sometimes of quarter-tone clusters, sometimes of semitone clusters.

The *Kyrie* is very much part of the Italian experience, being written during a time when I was reacting to the exposure to the great treasures of Italian art. The extensive use of gongs and reverberating instruments was certainly stimulated by the ever-present reverberation of bell sounds in Italy, though it was not my intention to reproduce them literally.

The *Kyrie* is a work of great stature and dignity.[8] Its effectiveness is due not only to a rich fabric of instrumental and vocal colours, but to the

8 The entire score of *Kyrie* is published in the Canadian literary quarterly *Exile* I, 3 (1973): 161–218.

skill with which Somers draws upon our collective memory of liturgy and sacred music, ranging from incantation to the trumpet sounding on the Day of Judgment (in the latter Somers was inspired by Michelangelo's *Last Judgment* in the Sistine Chapel). However, with a few exceptions, such as the choral chanting of Psalm 130 towards the end, references to a traditional musical treatment of the liturgy are abstract. The male chorus, for instance, twice builds dense clusters activated by syllabic chanting at thirteen different but simultaneous tempi. The chanting of unsynchronized male voices undoubtedly triggers our memory of the sounds of a choir reverberating through the spaces of a cathedral, yet in *Kyrie* the effect is to probe a different layer of meaning than would normally be aroused by a male choir singing a liturgical text. Similarly, at the opening of the work the many shades of emotion involved in supplication are evoked by the gradual intensification of a single soprano line consisting of colour changes on long sustained notes, slow trills on a minor second, speeding up and slowing down again, and a variety of glissandi. The emotional impact of this passage is intensified by the lack of a semantic text, the silences between phrases, and the extraordinary accompaniment of scraped gongs and tam-tam. At the end of *Kyrie* tension is resolved when the tenor solo sings the words 'Kyrie eleison' and 'Christe eleison,' accompanied by the choir chanting Psalm 130.

The listener will recognize many facets of Somers' language in *Kyrie*: the falling minor second (suggesting anguish and supplication); the gradual build-up to intense climaxes over a long arc; the multi-layered texture (as in the two passages for male chorus mentioned above); the gradual introduction of vocal and instrumental forces over the course of the work (comparable to the procedure in *Stereophony*); the use of brass instruments to heighten the intensity of climaxes (the entry of unison trumpets towards the climax of *Kyrie* recalls a similar procedure in the fugue in the Passacaglia and Fugue); and the evocative colours of low, reverberating percussion instruments (not unlike act II, scene ii of *Louis Riel*). *Kyrie* is the culmination of Somers' development during the sixties, in terms of both new vocal techniques and musical language. In this respect it occupies a position in his writing similar to that of the Symphony No. 1 to the works of the forties.

The other large scale vocal work, *Chura-churum*, was commissioned by the Montreal Symphony for the Swingle Singers, to be performed with the orchestra. It was begun early in 1972 and at the time of writing has not been completed. As noted earlier, Somers has described the work as a product of his visit to the East:

The basic word material is in Sanskrit, and is a 'puja' or prayer, in a sense. The title is taken from one of the words meaning 'All living non-living creation.'

In the piece I use the full range of vocal possibilities I had developed in *Voiceplay*, but here kept within a totally 'musical' concept as apart from the theatrical concept I used in *Voiceplay*.

Eight microphones are channelled to eight loud speakers situated around the hall, and part of the conception is the 'choreography' of the placement and movement of vocal sound around the hall.

I use a notational system developed from my work in schools, *Voiceplay*, and *Kyrie*. It also uses traditional notation when called for.

While continuing to explore in these vocal works the sophisticated notational techniques, sounds, and methods of organization of what has perhaps unfortunately become known as 'advanced' contemporary music, Somers has continued to write occasional music of a more accessible nature. In 1972 he provided the music for five one-hour programs in the CBC television series 'Images of Canada.' Concentrating on the social and economic rather than the political history of each region, the programs evoked, through imaginative use of paintings, drawings, graphics, on-the-scene camera work, and thoughtful narration, the various strands which shaped each region. That the sound-track of each program can be thoroughly enjoyed on its own, apart from the visual images, is no small measure of the richness of Somers' score. In order to prepare for the task he did extensive research into early Canadian musical repertoire – hymns, plain-chant, folk-songs – and was deeply impressed by the richness of this country's musical heritage, particularly that of Quebec (which can trace its musical ancestry back to Normandy, Brittany, and the Loire Valley). It is Somers' hope that this material, which so effectively creates the period and atmosphere of each program, will not only suggest areas for further research, but provide a small repertoire performable by students.

Of the five programs, the most complex, in terms of texture and density is 'The Magic Circle' (a portrait of New France, 1600–1867). The extensive use of collage techniques, as well as the great variety of sounds and musical material, creates a rich and evocative texture. In 'The Magic Circle' the instrumental music distinctly recalls the 'West' music of *Louis Riel* – sparse sleigh-bell rattles, sustained brass sonorities (with the characteristic crescendo dynamic envelope), drums, and solo flute (which, here as in *Riel*, often serves as a recurring element to bind together different sections, and even has a similar melodic profile). The bleak atmosphere created by these elements is at least partly balanced by choral music reminiscent of several Somers works of the sixties, in particular, the church scene in act III of *Louis Riel*.

Harry Somers and his wife live in Toronto's Rosedale district, in an elegantly remodelled house filled with paintings and other *objets d'art* reflecting the catholic tastes and world travels of both. In a midtown apartment building, Somers maintains a small studio, furnished with all the accoutrements of the composer's profession – a small upright piano, a handsome teak desk, bookshelves, a draughtsman's board (specially equipped with an instrument for drawing lines), copying pens, and comfortable chairs, all overlooked by one of Reginald Godden's mushroom spore prints.

Somers is a man of striking physical appearance – tall and lean, with a finely sculpted, sensitive face, highlighted by penetrating, clear eyes and light brown, slightly greying hair set back on a high forehead. There is a reserve, a philosophical detachment about him, especially when discussing his own work. Opinions are expressed, reflections ventured, all calmly and clearly articulated in an expressive, rich voice, punctuated by frequent flashes of humour and puffs on an ever-present pipe. One senses a private inner core, to be respected. Norma Beecroft, a friend and colleague for many years, has described him as 'a sensitive, generous, witty and alert individual, a stimulating conversationalist, keenly interested in most anyone and anything, a lover of life, of pipes and good wine, and good food.'[9] Another longtime friend, Victor Feldbrill, notes that while Somers is tolerant of human weakness, he 'doesn't suffer fools gladly.' Feldbrill recalls an incident which occurred some years ago, in which an instrumentalist who had given a bad performance of a work by Somers, breathlessly inquired of the composer whether he had heard the performance. 'Yes,' replied Somers, 'and don't ever touch my music again.'

To establish a relationship between the personality of a composer and the qualities of his music is troublesome in some cases, and probably futile in most. How to relate an individual, seemingly detached emotionally and guided by cool intellectual processes, to the emotional drive and intensity of so much of the music from the early forties through to the sixties? Feldbrill, who is perhaps best qualified to comment, notes that much of the music is characterized by long lines, on the surface highly controlled and often serene, yet 'underneath there is

9 'Musicscope' documentary 1972

something driving, an agitation.' This duality, observed Feldbrill, reflects the composer's appearance and personality – slender and calm, yet with a strong undercurrent of nervous excitement and energy.

The apposition of emotional drive and intellectual control has produced what is probably the most important single factor in Somers' music: tension, not necessarily in the sense of an overwhelming, constant presence, but as a basic compositional device, a means of imparting vitality and direction to a piece of music and, perhaps above all, a means of establishing a direct line of communication with the listener. As pointed out in this study, Somers has worked with tension in a number of ways: as a build-up and release of energy over wide areas in the course of an entire work or movement; in the use of extended line, with built-in tension-producing characteristics such as contour and tempo changes, often underlined by irregular, nervous accompaniment; in the contrapuntal procedures and style juxtaposition of the fifties; the use of multi-layered textures (which can be seen as recently as the *Kyrie*); and finally, the use of 'dynamic unrest.'

Together with this quality, Somers' music has a sense of forward thrust and energy, perhaps best expressed as an archetype which permeates much of his music of the fifties and early sixties, not only in a literal sense (for this figure recurs constantly) but in the sense of a basic pattern of growth, to be varied and permutated:[10]

A feeling of sheer physical energy arising from keenly honed elements of sound, cogently organized and not without dramatic propriety, can be detected immediately at the outset of the best and most characteristic works, for instance, *North Country*, the Violin Sonata No. 1, the String Quartet No. 3, or *Stereophony*. Yet one senses a streak of melancholy running through Somers' music, even a certain bleakness, which originates in spare, dissonant textures. These characteristics, in addition to the use of 'long, severe melodic lines'[11] are perhaps traits of a 'northern' composer, although attempts to establish such relationships are difficult and tend to obscure a thorough examination of the music itself.

In a country which has produced a sizable number of composers of stature during the past twenty years, Somers occupies a leading position

10 See, for example, the opening of Music for Solo Violin.
11 Schafer *Louis Riel: A Case Study* 17

as a major creative figure. In April of 1972 he was made a Companion of the Order of Canada, this country's highest award.[12]

This study has been a report on Harry Somers in mid-career – a composer of striking originality, imagination, and vitality, who continues to explore new areas of life and art with the same curiosity, open-mindedness, and intellectual vigour evident throughout his career.

In the end a work of art needs no justification; it is a phenomenon of the human mind and spirit which can, if we let it, if we take off our inhibiting blinkers, awaken us to vast areas of response which lie dormant within all of us, reveal the world in which we live, and, on occasion, afford us pleasure and entertainment on many levels.
Harry Somers, 'Music of Today' 1 April 1966

12 On 6 July 1973 Somers was the recipient of the University of Alberta's National Award in Music.

Compositions by Harry Somers*

TITLE, INSTRUMENTATION	PUBLISHER, DURATION, FIRST PERFORMANCE
1942	
Strangeness of Heart; pno	Berandol; 3′ 25″
1943	
String Quartet No. 1	CMC; 17′ 30″; Toronto 1945
Étude; pno	MS; 2′; Toronto 1945 (Reginald Godden)
1944	
Flights of Fancy; pno	MS; 8′; Toronto 1945 (R. Godden)
1 'Dance'	
2 'A Mood'	
3 'Moon Haze'	
Dark and Light; pno	MS; 1′ 20″; Toronto 1945 (R. Godden)
A fragment (became 2nd movement of *Testament of Youth*); pno	MS; 2′; Toronto 1945 (R. Godden)
1945	
Testament of Youth (Piano Sonata No. 1); pno	CMC; 13′; Toronto 1946 (R. Godden)

*This list does not include juvenilia mentioned in the text.

1946
Three Songs (Walt Whitman);
voice, pno
1 'Look Down, Fair Moon'
2 'After the Dazzle of Day'
3 'A Clear Midnight'

CMC; 6' 20"; Toronto 1946
(Frances James); commissioned
by Forest Hill Community
Centre

Slow Movement for Strings (2nd
movement of String Quartet
No. 1); string orch

MS; 5'; 1946

Sketches for Orchestra; full orch
1 'Horizon'
2 'Shadows'
3 'West Wind'

MS; 14'; 'Shadows': Toronto
1947 (CBC: Sir Bernard Heinze,
cond); remainder: Eastman
School Rochester 1948 (Howard
Hanson, cond)

Three Sonnets; pno
1 'Prelude'
2 'Lullaby to a Dead Child'
3 'Primeval'

Berandol; 9'; Toronto 1948
(composer)

Piano Sonata No. 2; pno

CMC; 20'; Toronto 1948 (composer)

1947
Scherzo for Strings; string orch

Associated Music Publishers; 5';
Toronto 1947 (CBC: Harold
Sumberg, cond)

Solitudes; pno
1 Lento
2 Largo
3 Andante
4 Allegro molto

MS; 10'; Toronto 1948 (composer)

Piano Concerto No. 1; pno, full
orch

MS; 25'; Toronto 1949 (Conservatory Orchestra; Ettore Mazzoleni, cond; composer, pno)

Suite for Percussion; pno,
4 drums
1 'Declamation'
2 'Fughetta'

MS; Arts and Letters Club, Toronto 1947 (R. Godden, pno;
composer and others, perc)

TITLE, INSTRUMENTATION	PUBLISHER, DURATION, FIRST PERFORMANCE

3 'A Bit of Dust'
4 'Adagio'
5 'Fast Bues'

A Song of Joys; medium voice, pno
MS; 4'

A Bunch of Rowan (Diana Skala); medium voice, pno
Berandol; 4'; World Youth Festival, Budapest 1949

1948

Rhapsody for Violin and Piano; vln, pno
CMC; 9'; Toronto 1948 (Morry Kernerman, vln; composer, pno)

Woodwind Quintet; fl, ob, cl, bn, hn
MS; 24'

North Country; string orch
Berandol; 12' 48"; Toronto 1948 (CBC: Geoffrey Waddington, cond)

Mime; vln, pno
MS; 5'; Toronto (CBC: M. Kernerman, vln; composer, pno)

1949

Four Primitives; pno
MS; 9'

Suite for Harp and Chamber Orchestra; fl, ob, cl, bn, solo harp, string orch
Berandol; 22' 50"; Canadian League of Composers Concert, Toronto 1952 (B. Heinze, cond; Marie Iosch, harp)

1950

String Quartet No. 2
CMC; 25' 20"; Toronto 1963 (Canadian String Quartet)

Piano Sonata No. 3; pno
CMC; 24'; Montreal 1957 (CBC: Samuel Levitan, pno)

Piano Sonata No. 4; pno
CMC; 15'; Paris 1950 (Eugene Gash, pno)

Trio; fl, vln, vlc
CMC; 12'

TITLE, INSTRUMENTATION	PUBLISHER, DURATION, FIRST PERFORMANCE
The Case of the Wayward Woodwinds; chamber orch	MS; 5'; Toronto 1951 (CBC: John Adaskin, cond); commissioned by the CBC for 'Opportunity Knocks' (J. Adaskin)

1951

Symphony No. 1; full orch	Berandol; 28'; Toronto 1953 (CBC Symphony Orchestra, Victor Feldbrill, cond)
12 x 12 (Fugues for piano); pno	Berandol; 15'
Lament and *Primeval* (orchestration of the last two of the Three Sonnets); full orch	CMC; 5'; Toronto 1952 (Varsity Stadium Ballet, V. Feldbrill, cond); commissioned by the National Film Board (Louis Applebaum)

1952

Prelude and Fugue for Orchestra; full orch	5'; Toronto 1952 (CBC: J. Adaskin, cond); commissioned by the CBC for 'Opportunity Knocks' (J. Adaskin)

1953

The Fool (Michael Fram); 4 soloists (SATB), wind and str qt, d bs, pno	CMC; 50'; Toronto 1956 (V. Feldbrill, cond; H. Geiger-Torel, stage director)
Sonata No. 1 for Violin and Piano; vln, pno	Berandol; 23' 35"; Stratford Festival 1955 (Hyman Goodman, vln; Leo Barkin, pno)
Three Simple Songs (Michael Fram); mez sop 1 'The Garden' 2 'Asleep' 3 'My Faith Moves Mountains'	CMC; 6'; Canadian League of Composers Concert, Hamilton 1954 (Trudy Carlyle, mez sop; Mario Bernardi, pno)

1954

Passacaglia and Fugue for Orchestra; full orch	Berandol; 11' 15"; Toronto 1954 (CBC Symphony Orchestra, E. Mazzoleni, cond)

TITLE, INSTRUMENTATION	PUBLISHER, DURATION, FIRST PERFORMANCE

1955

Sonata No. 2 for Violin and Piano; vln, pno — Berandol; 15'; Toronto 1955 (Jacob Groob, vln; composer, pno)

Where Do We Stand, Oh Lord? (Michael Fram); chorus (SATB) — Berandol; 8' 22"; Hamilton 1955 (Collegium Musicum, Udo Kasemets, cond)

Conversation Piece (Michael Fram); high voice, pno — Berandol; 2' 30"; Toronto 1956

Two Songs for the Coming of Spring (Michael Fram); chorus (SATB) 1 'Winter, Will You Not Go?' 2 'Winter's Over, Spring's Begun' — Berandol; 2' 15"; Ontario Music Educators' Association Convention, Toronto 1957

The Homeless Ones (television operetta, Michael Fram); narrator, voices, orch — MS; 12'; CBC TV, Toronto 1956; commissioned by CBC TV

Little Suite for String Orchestra on Canadian Folk Songs; string orch — Berandol; 7'; Toronto 1956 (Bennington Heights Community Orchestra); commissioned by Alumni Association of the Faculty of Music of the University of Toronto

1956

Piano Concerto No. 2; solo pno, full orch — Berandol; 43'; Toronto 1956 (CBC Symphony Orchestra, V. Feldbrill, cond; R. Godden, pno)

Five Songs for Dark Voice (Michael Fram); contralto, chamber orch — Berandol (pno-vocal score); 11' 50"; Stratford, Ontario 1956 (Maureen Forrester, contralto); commissioned by the Stratford Festival

The Fisherman and His Soul (ballet based on story by Oscar Wilde; choreography, Grant Strate); full orch — MS; 28'; Hamilton 1956; commissioned by the National Ballet of Canada

160 Harry Somers

TITLE, INSTRUMENTATION	PUBLISHER, DURATION, FIRST PERFORMANCE
Faces of Canada (incidental music); full orch	MS; 25'; Toronto 1956; commissioned by CBC TV
1957 Movement for Woodwind Quintet	MS; 6'
Piano Sonata No. 5	CMC; 15'
1958 Fantasia for Orchestra; full orch	Berandol; 12'; Montreal 1958 (Montreal Symphony Orchestra, Igor Markevitch, cond); commissioned by the Junior Committee of the Montreal Symphony Orchestra
Ballad (ballet; choreography, Grant Strate); full orch	MS; 29'; Ottawa 1958 (National Ballet of Canada); commissioned by the National Ballet of Canada
1959 String Quartet No. 3	CMC; 22'; Vancouver 1959 (Hungarian String Quartet); commissioned by the Vancouver Festival Society for the Hungarian String Quartet
Sonata for Guitar	E.C. Kerby; 10' 30"; Toronto 1964 (Peter Acker); commissioned by the Guitar Society of Toronto
1959–60 *Saguenay* (film score); chamber orch	MS; 14'; commissioned by Alcan Ltd
1960 *Lyric* for Orchestra; full orch	Berandol; 7' 30"; Washington

TITLE, INSTRUMENTATION

PUBLISHER, DURATION, FIRST
PERFORMANCE

1961 (Orquesta Sinfónica Na-
cional de México, L.H. de la
Fuente, cond); commissioned
by the Serge Koussevitzky
Music Foundation in the Library of Congress

1961
Symphony for Woodwinds,
Brass and Percussion

Peters; 17' 45"; Pittsburgh 1961
(Pittsburgh Wind Symphony,
Robert Boudreau, cond); com-
missioned by the Pittsburgh
Wind Symphony

Five Concepts for Orchestra;
full orch

Berandol; 23'; Toronto 1962
(CBC Symphony Orchestra, G.
Waddington, cond)

1962
Movement (formerly Abstract
for Television); full orch

Ricordi; 10'; Toronto 1962 (CBC
TV Orchestra, M. Bernardi,
cond); commissioned by CBC TV
MS

At the Descent from the Cross; 2
guitars, bass voice
God, The Master of this Scene
(words adapted from Jeremy
Taylor by Bruce Attridge);
chorus (SATB)

G.V. Thompson; 3' 35"; Toronto
1962; commissioned by John
Roberts

Gloria; chorus (SATB), 2 trpts,
org

G.V. Thompson; 3'; Toronto
1962; commissioned by CBC TV

1963
The House of Atreus (ballet;
choreography, Grant Strate);
full orch or chamber orch

MS; 31'; Toronto 1964 (National
Ballet of Canada); commis-
sioned by the National Ballet of
Canada

Stereophony; full orch

E.C. Kerby; 17'; Toronto 1963
(Toronto Symphony Orchestra,

162 Harry Somers

TITLE, INSTRUMENTATION	PUBLISHER, DURATION, FIRST PERFORMANCE
Twelve Miniatures (Haiku, trans. Harold G. Henderson); sop, rec or fl, vla da gamba or vlc, spinet or pno	Walter Susskind, cond); commissioned by the Toronto Symphony Orchestra Berandol; 15′; CBC radio 1964 (Mary Morrison, sop; Nicholas Fiore, fl; Walter Buczynski, spinet; Donald Whitton, vlc); commissioned by the CBC

1964

Theme for Variations; any combination of instruments	Berandol; 3′ 5″; Toronto 1965 (school group); commissioned by the Canadian Music Centre (John Adaskin Project)
Picasso (documentary score); small inst group	MS; CBC TV 1964 (Vincent Torell, producer)
Picasso Suite; small orch	Ricordi; 19′ 15″; Saskatoon 1965 (Saskatoon Symphony Orchestra, David Kaplan, cond); commissioned by the Saskatoon Symphony Orchestra
Etching – The Vollard Suite (from Picasso Suite); fl	Ricordi; 2′ 30″; Saskatoon 1965 (Saskatoon Symphony Orchestra, David Kaplan, cond); commissioned by the Saskatoon Symphony Orchestra
The Wonder Song; chorus (SATB)	Berandol; 4′; Toronto 1965 (choir of Riverdale Collegiate, John Ford, cond); commissioned by the Canadian Music Centre

1965

The Gift	MS; 60 ′; Toronto 1965 (CBC); commissioned by CBC TV

TITLE, INSTRUMENTATION

PUBLISHER, DURATION, FIRST
PERFORMANCE

1966
Crucifixion; chorus (SATB), Eng
hn, 2 trpts, harp, perc

MS; 6'; 1966 (CBC TV; Festival
Singers of Canada, Elmer Iseler,
cond)

Evocations (Harry Somers);
mez sop, pno

Berandol; 15' 15"; 1967 (CBC
radio; Patricia Rideout, mez
sop; composer, pno); commissioned by the CBC

1967
Louis Riel (libretto, Mavor
Moore, Jacques Languirand);
cast of 37 (26 soloists, SATB
choir), full orch, prepared tape

MS; 2 hours 13'; Toronto, 23 September 1967 (V. Feldbrill,
cond; Leon Major, stage director); commissioned by the
Floyd Chalmers Foundation

Kuyas (adapted from *Louis
Riel*); sop, fl, perc

Berandol; 7' 15"; Toronto 1967;
commissioned by Institut International de Musique du
Canada

1968
Improvisation; narrator,
singers (SATB), str, ww (any
number), 2 perc, 1 pianist (2
pno), cond

MS; 10' 15"; CBC Montreal Festival, 1968; commissioned by the
CBC

1969
Five Songs of the Newfoundland
Outports (collected by Kenneth Peacock); chorus (SATB),
pno
1 'Si j'avais le bateau'
2 'The Banks of Newfoundland'
3 'The Old "Mayflower"'

G.V. Thompson; 19'; Toronto
1969 (Festival Singers of
Canada, E. Iseler, cond); commissioned by the CBC

TITLE, INSTRUMENTATION	PUBLISHER, DURATION, FIRST PERFORMANCE

4 'She's Like the Swallow'
5 'Feller from Fortune'
And; dancers, SATB soloists, fl,
harp, pno, 4 perc

MS; 35–40 '; Toronto 1969 (CBC TV, Toronto Dance Theatre); commissioned by CBC TV

1971
Voiceplay; 1 singer/actor

CMC; 15–20 '; Toronto 1972 (Cathy Berberian); commissioned by the CBC

1972
Kyrie; SATB soloists, chorus, fl, ob, cl, vlc, 3 trpts, pno, 6 perc

Published in *Exile: A Literary Quarterly*, 1, 3 (1973): 161–218; 25 '; Toronto 1974 (Roxolana Roslak, sop; Festival Singers of Canada, instrumental ensemble, E. Iseler, cond); commissioned by CBC TV

1972–3
Images of Canada (5 one-hour programs); varied ensembles

MS; 5 hours; 1973–4, CBC TV; commissioned by CBC TV

1973
Chura-churum; 8 voices, orch (in progress)

MS; 27 '; commissioned by the Montreal Symphony Orchestra for the Swingle Singers

Music for Solo Violin

CMC; 21 ' 30 "; Guelph, Ontario 1974 (Yehudi Menuhin); commissioned by Yehudi Menuhin (with the Canada Council and the Guelph Spring Festival)

CMC   Canadian Music Centre

Discography

TITLE, ARTISTS	RECORD NUMBER
Etching – The Vollard Suite; Jadwiga Michalska, fl	SM-114
Fantasia for Orchestra; Montreal Symphony Orchestra, Pierre Hétu, cond	RCA LSC-2980
Five Songs for Dark Voice; Maureen Forrester, contr; National Arts Centre Orchestra, Mario Bernardi, cond	RCA LSC-3172
Five Songs of the Newfoundland Outports; Festival Singers of Canada, Elmer Iseler, cond; George Brough, pno	RCA LSC-3154
The Fool; Roxolana Roslak, sopr; Patricia Rideout, contr; David Astor, tenor; Maurice Brown, bass; instrumental ensemble, Victor Feldbrill, cond	RCA LSC-3094
Gloria; Toronto Mendelssohn Choir, Joseph Umbrico and Ronald Neal, trpts; George Brough, organ; E. Iseler, cond	RCA LSC-3054
God, The Master of this Scene; Festival Singers of Canada, E. Iseler, cond	Cap ST-6258
Music for Solo Violin; Yehudi Menuhin, vln	CBC RCI 413
North Country; CBC String Orchestra, Paul Scherman, cond	CBC RCI 154

Passacaglia and Fugue; Louisville Orchestra,	Lou 661
Robert Whitney, cond	Lou LS 661
Piano Sonata No. 3; André-Sébastien Savoie	CBC RCI 251
Piano Sonata No. 5, slow movement; Walter	SM-162
Buczynski	
Piano Sonata No. 5; Antonin Kubalek	Melbourne
	SMLP-4023
Rhapsody for Violin and Piano; Duo Pach:	CBC RCI 244
Joseph Pach, vln; Arlene Nimmons, pno	
Scherzo for Strings; Toronto Symphony	CBC RCI 41
Orchestra, Sir Ernest MacMillan, cond	
Scherzo for Strings; Hart House Orchestra, Boyd	CBC RCI 238
Neel, cond	
Sketches for Orchestra; Orchestre de Radio-	CBC RCI 88
Canada à Montréal, Roland Leduc, cond	
Sonata No. 1 for Violin and Piano; Marta Hidy,	RCA CC/CCS-1015
vln; Chester Duncan, pno	
Sonata No. 2 for Violin and Piano; Steven	RCA CC/CCS-1016
Staryk, vln; Lise Boucher, pno	
Strangeness of Heart; Ross Pratt, pno	CBC RCI 93
Strangeness of Heart; Ross Pratt, pno	CBC RCI 132
Suite for Harp and Chamber Orchestra; CBC	Col ML-5685
Symphony Orchestra, Judy Loman, harp;	Col MS-6285
Walter Susskind, cond	
Symphony for Winds, Brass and Percussion; CBC	SM-134
Wind Symphony, Victor Feldbrill, cond	
Twelve Miniatures; Mary Morrison, sopr;	RCA CC/CCS-1011
Nicholas Fiore, fl; Walter Buczynski, spinet;	
Donald Whitton, cello	
Two songs for the Coming of Spring; Montreal	CBC RCI 206
Bach Choir, George Little, cond	
Where Do We Stand, Oh Lord?; CBC Choir,	CBC RCI 130
Geoffrey Waddington, cond	

KEY

Cap	Capitol	Lou	Louisville
CBC RCI	CBC Radio-Canada	RCA	RCA Victor
	International	SM	CBC Canadian Collection
Col	Columbia		

Synopsis of *Louis Riel*

Historical background: In 1867 Canada was born from a union of Ontario and Quebec with the maritime provinces of Nova Scotia and New Brunswick. In the same year, the Hudson's Bay Company, holding administrative power in the mid-west under British charter, changed hands – and the new owners proved as anxious to sell the territory as Canada was to acquire it. Consequently, in 1869 the new Canadian parliament passed legislation for the future government of Rupert's Land and the North-West Territory, to take effect when ratified by Britain.

In this transaction the settlers already in the area – British, French, Irish, half-breeds, and others – were not consulted, and were to receive no recompense for their land. The proposed legislation set up a Crown Colony in which settlers would have no rights of citizenship – a prospect which deeply concerned those of French origin. When the Canadian government tactlessly sent out surveyors to mark off the land even before the transfer of authority, and the lame-duck Hudson's Bay Company administration faltered, the alarmed Red River settlers set up their own provisional government, owing allegiance to the Queen alone, in hopes of negotiating better terms before joining Canada.

While recognizing this step as legal under the Law of Nations, the Canadian government in Ottawa proceeded to appoint a governor, William McDougall, and despatched him via Minnesota to await, just south of the border, the expected proclamation from the Queen. The anti-French, anti-catholic McDougall grew impatient, and in November 1869 he tried to enter the territory with a forged proclamation.

It is at this point that the action of the opera begins, and history becomes subject to dramatic licence.

Mavor Moore in the 1967 program of the World Festival, Montreal

Note: 'atonal' is used to refer to the music of the West; → = progression from one style to another; + = superimposition of two styles.

SETTING	PLOT	TYPE OF MUSIC
ACT I		
Introduction		Percussion improvisation (timpani and tom-toms), → song 'Riel Sits in His Chamber o'State'; → atonal orchestral music and electronic sounds
Scene i u.s.–Canadian border, south of Fort Garry, 1869	McDougall and his retinue are stopped and prevented from crossing the border by a band of Métis. Thomas Scott, a violently fanatic Orangeman scout, attacks the Métis and is arrested.	Atonal (beginning thin texture, building to climax with chorus of Métis, fuller texture) → return of 'Riel Sits in His Chamber,' in violins, with percussion improvisation
Scene ii Fort Garry, Red River headquarters of the Hudson's Bay Company	Riel and his followers have taken over the fort. After a heated confrontation with Riel, Dr Schultz and Charles Mair, leaders of the 'Canadian faction,' leave. Riel prays for divine guidance. When Scott is brought in, Riel lets him go (against the advice of his followers) on condition he keep the peace. Instead Scott joins Mair and Schultz.	Atonal (fanfare-like music in brass and drums; thin orchestral support for voices) → flute solo (based on Riel's song) becomes motivic basis of Riel's soliloquy → return of atonal music and Métis chorus 'Le Roi malheureux' → Métis chorus 'Est-il rien sur la terre?' with atonal-style support from brass and percussion
Scene iii The Prime Minister's office, Ottawa	Macdonald, Cartier, and Donald Smith receive Bishop Taché, a spokesman and go-between for the rebels. Macdonald assures him that the province of Manitoba will be set up and an amnesty given to Riel. McDougall is severely reprimanded. Smith is sent west to 'sugar' the situation (make promises to the Métis).	'Sir John-slightly-high' music → atonal (during exchange with McDougall) → 'sugar' aria (Sir John as vaudeville singer)

SETTING	PLOT	TYPE OF MUSIC
Scene iv The house of Julie Riel	Riel completes the Manitoba constitution for Taché to take back to Ottawa. In a soliloquy, Riel recalls a psalm of David and envisions himself as David's reincarnation called by God to lead his people.	Atonal (thin support for dialogue between Julie, Taché, Riel) → Riel's soliloquy (score indicates accompaniment by electronic sounds)
ACT II		
Scene i The Prime Minister's office, Ottawa	Taché, Macdonald, and Cartier discuss the terms under which Manitoba will enter Confeder- ation, including certain rights such as French in court and Catholic schools. Macdonald promises Taché an amnesty will be given to Riel but later tells Cartier that they must not grant it, since an election is coming up.	'Sir-John-slightly-high' music (especially in orchestral intro- duction and fragments of 'atonal' music)
Scene ii Fort Garry	Scott is tried for treason and condemned to death. The trial is very irregular (for example, there are only six in the jury, all of whom are French- speaking). Riel explains that he 'cannot let one foolish man stand in the way of a whole na- tion' but later admits that he hates Scott because he is 'full of evil.'	Atonal (gong sounds, percus- sion – sparse texture for build- ing suspense) → Métis chorus 'Est-il rien sur la terre?' + atonal music (derived from percussion material beginning of act I, scene i)
Scene iii Fort Garry, the day of Scott's execution	Sara and Julie Riel (sister and mother) plead with Riel to spare Scott's life. Riel refuses ('It is God himself who guides my hand'). Scott is executed.	Atonal (one long crescendo, from thin texture at the open- ing to full tutti – unison rhyth- mic declamations against sus- tained strings)

SETTING	PLOT	TYPE OF MUSIC
Scene iv A railway depot, Toronto	Schultz and Mair harangue the crowd, showing them relics of the late Thomas Scott. As a martyr to the cause of Ontario Orangemen, Scott is a useful figure now (Schultz: 'Thomas Scott alive was a pain in every ass, but his corpse'll be a hero by and by').	Diatonic 'hymn-tune' music ('Canada first; Canada is British. Oh Or'ngemen unite') → Victorian tune (on cornet) + 'We'll Hang Him up the River'
Scene v The Prime Minister's office, Ottawa	Macdonald's cabinet is split; was Scott's execution a legal act or murder? Colonel Wolseley wants to march on Fort Garry but Cartier warns that Quebec will rise if he does. Macdonald suggests that the army go to keep the peace until a new governor, Archibald, arrives with the amnesty and Riel resigns, as promised. Taché goes to assure Riel all is well.	Various thematic elements of earlier Ottawa scenes; several new motives introduced
Scene vi The courtyard, Fort Garry	Riel's followers (chiefly O'Donaghue) suspect the intentions of Wolseley's forces, but are mollified by a proclamation stating that his mission is merely to keep the peace. However, Riel and his followers are tricked into fleeing by false reports of the approaching army's intention to hang Riel. Wolseley takes over the town.	Two dances (including 'The Buffalo Hunt'); atonal music of the West: short, nervous rhythmic fragments + 'We'll Hang Him up the River' (sung off-stage by approaching troops)
ACT III		
Scene i Riel's house, Sun River, Montana, 1880	Riel, in exile, is a schoolteacher with an Indian wife and infant son. A deputation arrives from Saskatchewan to recruit Riel to lead a rebellion there. Above the protestations of his wife, Riel finally agrees to go along.	Marguerite's solo aria 'Kuyas' (from a Tsimshian Indian song) → atonal music + material from 'Kuyas'; building to thick texture, then thinning to drums, sleigh-bells, etc.

SETTING	PLOT	TYPE OF MUSIC
Scene ii Prime Minister's office, Ottawa	Macdonald calls upon Taché to help put down the rebels by refusing the sacrament to anyone taking up arms. He assures Taché that the police will only be peacekeepers, but orders an army to be mobilized and ready to march west.	Ottawa music of earlier scenes; thin, accompaniment texture
Scene iii A church, Frog Lake, Saskatchewan, 1885	Father André is celebrating mass. He is interrupted by the appearance of a band of Indians, then by Riel, who accuses the priest of selling out to enemies, then takes possession of the church. Riel tells of a dream, prophesying the arrival of an army from the east. This turns out to be true and the people proclaim him to be a prophet.	Latin, plainsong-style chant of church service → return of atonal music of act I, scene i, but expanded → ends with flute solo first heard in act I, scene ii
Interlude	(Battle)	Repeat of introduction to opera (electronic, and atonal, orchestral)
Scene iv The courtroom, Regina	The Métis have been defeated by a federal army and Riel is on trial for high treason. Friends in Quebec have sent lawyers to prove him insane; the Crown intends to prove him sane and guilty.	Atonal music: many layers of events – choral shouting, nervous rhythmic fragments, long lines in strings moving simultaneously in half-notes
Scene v Riel's cell	Riel's mother Julie reassures him that nothing can happen so long as he retains faith in God.	Very sparse atonal; suggestions in Julie's part of elements of the earlier song 'Riel Sits in His Chamber'

SETTING	PLOT	TYPE OF MUSIC
Scene vi The courtroom, Regina	Riel takes over his own defence. He pleads that he should be ac- quitted because he acted 'against a government gone mad.' The Crown lawyer, Osler, declines to address the jury since Riel has proved him- self sane by speaking so lucidly and eloquently.	Solo aria, unaccompanied
Scene vii A street, Ottawa	Taché and Lemieux plead with Macdonald for a reprieve for Riel. Macdonald replies 'I can- not let one foolish man stand in the way of a whole nation.'	Elements of earlier Ottawa music, now the basis of more continuous, tenser texture building to massive tutti (in- cluding taped chorus). Opera ends with flute solo from act I, scene ii

Selected bibliography

ANON. 'The CBC Symphony with a New Canadian Work: the First Symphony by Harry Somers' *CBC Times* 26 April–2 May 1953, 3
- *Composers of the Americas* vol. 5, Washington, Pan American Union 1959
- 'The Fool' *CBC Times* 11–17 December 1965, 11
- 'Harry Somers' *The Music Scene* September–October 1967, 7
- 'Harry Somers' BMI Canada Ltd. n.d. (ten-page pamphlet containing critico-biographical essay, excerpts from reviews, and a selective list of works)
- 'Harry Somers: A Portrait' *Musicanada* 4 (September 1967): 8–9
ARTHUR, F. 'Somers in Recital of Own Works' *Saturday Night* 20 March 1948, 34
BECKWITH, JOHN 'Composers in Toronto and Montreal' *University of Toronto Quarterly* 26 (October 1956): 47–69
- 'Harry Somers' in *Dictionary of Contemporary Music* edited by John Vinton, New York, E.P. Dutton & Co. 1974
BUTLER, E. GREGORY *The Piano Sonatas of Harry Somers* AMD dissertation in progress, University of Rochester
DESAUTELS, ANDRÉE 'The History of Canadian Composition 1610–1967' in *Aspects of Music in Canada* edited by Arnold Walter, Toronto, University of Toronto Press 1969, 124–6
FERRY, A. 'Harry Somers: A Composer, TV Teacher, Beachcomber on the Fringe of Art' *Maclean's* 1 June 1963, 62

GRAHAM, JUNE 'Louis Riel' CBC Times 25–31 October 1967, 2–6
– 'A Harry Somers Evening' CBC Times 17–23 August 1968, 4–5
HEPNER, LEE 'An Analytical Study of Selected Canadian Orchestral
  Compositions at the Mid-Twentieth Century' PH D dissertation, New
  York University 1971
HUDSON, RICHARD 'Canadian Contrasts' Ricordiana 10 (October 1965):
  1–3
KALLMANN, HELMUT (ed.) Catalogue of Canadian Composers rev. ed.
  Toronto, CBC 1952
LITTLER, WILLIAM 'Italy's Cultural Shock Brought Composer to Life' The
  Toronto Daily Star 1 April 1972, 55
LORANGER, PIERRE 'Harry Somers: "The Picasso Suite"' The Canada
  Music Book 1 (Spring-Summer 1970): 145–52
MACNIVEN, ELINA 'Louis Riel' Opera Canada 8 (September 1967): 42
MCLEAN, ERIC 'Harry Somers: "The Fool"' The Canada Music Book 1
  (Spring-Summer 1970): 157–60
MOORE, MAVOR 'Why Louis Riel?' Opera Canada 7 (May 1966): 9
MOREY, CARL 'Canadian Opera?' Canadian Forum 48 (December 1968):
  206
OLNICK, HARVEY 'Harry Somers' The Canadian Music Journal 3 (Summer
  1959): 3–23
RAJEWSKY, V.I. 'Harry Somers' in Thirty-four Biographies of Canadian
  Composers Montreal, CBC International Service 1964; reprint ed., St
  Clair Shores, Mich., Scholarly Press 1972
ROSENTHAL, HAROLD 'Harold Rosenthal Reports from Canada' Opera 18
  (November 1967): 865–7
SCHAFER, R. MURRAY The Public of the Music Theatre: Louis Riel: A Case
  Study Vienna, Universal Edition 1972
SMITH, FRANCES An Analysis of Selected Works by Harry Somers M MUS
  thesis, University of Western Ontario 1973
SOMERS, HARRY 'The Agony of Maurice Lowe: A Reply' Canadian Forum
  35 (September 1955): 137–8
– Analysis of Suite for Harp and Chamber Orchestra Canadian Music
  Centre Study Course, no. 1, Toronto, Canadian Music Centre 1961
– 'Stereophony for Orchestra' Music Across Canada 1 (March 1963):
  27–8 (reprinted in the preface to the published score)
– 'Louis Riel: the Score' Opera Canada 8 (September 1967): 46
– 'Composer in the School: A Composer's View' Musicanada 19 (May
  1969): 7–9, 13–16

- 'A Letter from Rome' *The Canada Music Book* 1 (Spring-Summer 1970): 105–8
- 'Harry Somers' Letter to Lee Hepner' *The Canada Music Book* 3 (Autumn-Winter 1971): 87–97

SUCH, PETER 'Harry Somers' in *Soundprints* Toronto. Clarke, Irwin 1972, 30–53

WILSON, M. 'Music Review' (Somers' Piano Concerto No. 2) *Canadian Forum* 36 (April 1956): 15–16

WINTERS, KENNETH 'Somers: In the Spring of His Career' *The Toronto Telegram* 5 July 1969, 2

Index

References to musical examples are printed in boldface type.